Confidential Recollections Revealed

Gustave-Lambert Brahy

Translated from the French
by
James Herschel Holden, M.A.
Fellow of the
American Federation of Astrologers

ISBN-10: 0-86690-570-7
ISBN-13: 978-0-86690-570-1

Cover Design: Jack Cipolla

Published by:
American Federation of Astrologers, Inc.
6535 S. Rural Road
Tempe, AZ 85283

Printed in the United States of America

*The Author at the Astrological Conference
in New York in 1937.*

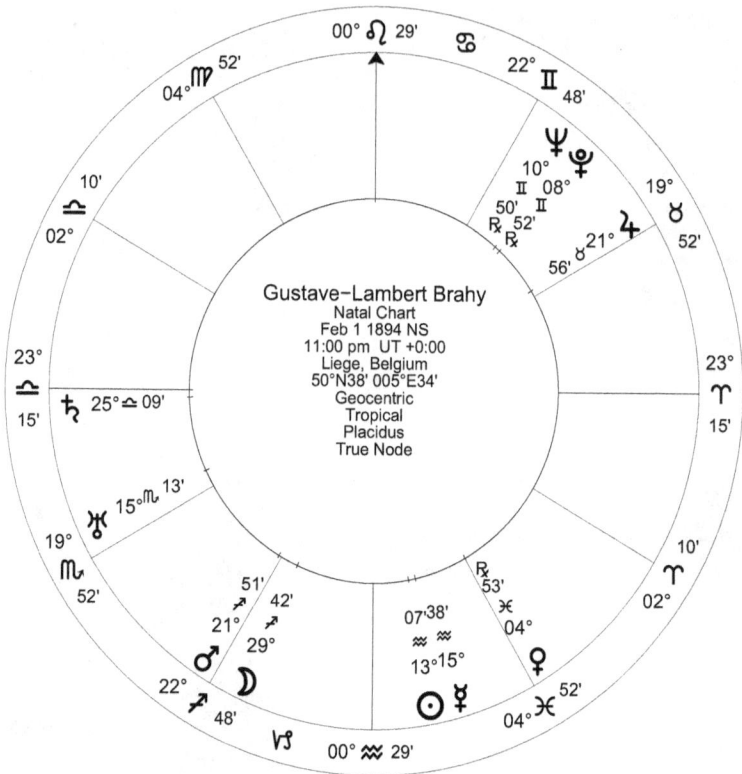

Gustave–Lambert Brahy
Natal Chart
Feb 1 1894 NS
11:00 pm UT +0:00
Liege, Belgium
50°N38' 005°E34'
Geocentric
Tropical
Placidus
True Node

Gustave-Lambert Brahy
Liège, Belgium 50N38 5E35
1 February 1894 11:00 PM

DEDICATION BY THE AUTHOR

To the fine and noble figure, Viscount
Charles de Herbais de Thun, who
with an absolute unselfishness, struggled
by my side during more than fifteen
years for the advancement of astrology.

The present volume is an English translation of the book:
Brahy, Gustave-Lambert
Confidences d'un Astrologue.
Brussels: Editions Flandre-Artois, 1946.

WORKS BY THE SAME AUTHOR

En Touriste aux Etats-Unis, a novel about a trip to the U.S. (11th thousand)
[On Tour in the United States]

Le Guardien du Seuil, an occult novel (3rd thousand)
[The Guardian of the Threshold]

Lueurs sur l'Inconnaissable (La Mort, l'Au-Delà, et la possibilité d'autres mondes et de vies futures). (3rd thousand)
[Glimpses of the Unknowable: Death, the Beyond, and the Possibility of Other Worlds and Future Lives]

Un Drame chez les Spirites, drame en 3 actes.
[A Drama among the Spirits, a drama in 3 acts]

Contribution à l'Etude de l'Astro-Dynamique (out of print)
[A Contribution to the Study of Astro-Dynamics]

La Nuit d'Ortygie, 3 stories. (out of print)
[The Night of Ortygia]

La Poème des Mains, poems in prose (out of print)
[The Poem of the Hands]

Le Mystère des Influences astrales (Illusions et Réalités) La véritable figure de l'astrologie (2nd thousand)
[The Mystery of Astral Influences (Illusions and Realities) The true Character of Astrology]

Sous quelle Etoile êtes-vous né? (4th thousand)
[Under what Star were you Born ?]

Soyez, vous aussi, Astrologue? (Méthode expresse pour apprendre à dresser et à interpréter synthétiquement un ciel de naissance). (2nd edition)
[Can you too be an Astrologer ? An express method to learn how to cast and interpret a natal chart]

Fluctuations boursières et Influences cosmiques (la Détermination des Fluctuations probables des Valeurs au moyen d'Astrologie). (2nd edition)
[Market fluctuations and Cosmic Influences (The Determination of Probable Fluctuations in Prices by means of Astrology]

TRANSLATIONS

From the English novelist Sir E. Bulwer-Lytton:
La Race qui nous exterminera (*The Coming Race*), a fantasy novel.
Zanoni, a novel about initiates.

TABLE OF CONTENTS

Translator's Preface

Gustave-Lambert Brahy (1894-1989) was perhaps the leading Belgian astrologer during the late 1920s, the 1930s, and the 1940s. His *Confidences* provide not only a fascinating account of his own life but also many interesting glimpses into the events that swirled around him as the European astrologers struggled with trying to form international associations. In 1926 he founded and served as its first director the Astrological Institute of Belgium. He was also an occultist and the founder of the Brussels Rosicrucian Center in 1935. In 1937 he spent more than a month in the United States, attending first the Convention organized by Adrian Ziegler (1891-1966) in New York City in May of that year, then touring the U.S., visiting the Rosicrucian Headquarters at Oceanside, California,[1] and returning to Europe in time to attend the Fourth International Astrological Convention in Paris in July, of which he gives an enlightening account.

His book also offers many insights into the activities of a professional astrologer, as well as his considered opinions on the state of astrology in the first year after World War II and its prospects for improvement in the post-war era.

Brahy was an excellent writer and stylist with a colorful vocabulary. In this translation I have somewhat dulled his style and perhaps not always rendered adequately some of his more subtle or idiomatic expressions. Where possible I have avoided paraphrase and tried to produce a fairly literal translation. I hope that if he

---

[1] The headquarters of the organization founded by Max Heindel and now known as the Rosicrucian Fellowship.

were able to read it, he would not be too dissatisfied with this English version of his book.

At the appropriate point in the text I have added Brahy's horoscope, which is not given in the book, although he does give his birth data. It is perhaps interesting to note that if the correction for parallax is applied to the position of his Moon, it would be in 0 ♑ 01 instead of 29 ♐ 42. I am inclined to think that Moon in Capricorn better suits his personality than Moon in Sagittarius, but I leave it to the astrological reader to decide which of the two positions seems to him be more indicative of Brahy's personality.

J.H.H.
7 September 2004

By Way of a Preface.

I have often been told:

"You should write your memoirs. Placed as you have been at the center of the Belgian astrological movement and in constant contact with the international movement, of which you have approached nearly all the most representative figures of our science; you have certainly acquired an extensive and almost unique experience."

"In addition, having created a movement, which, not being able to count on any official support, has had to find in itself its own means of existence and development, you have been able to appraise public reactions from all angles. You are therefore admirably placed to state the true situation, now that you have incontestably arrived at a plateau of the bold experience that you have undertaken. No one could speak to us better than you about the astrological movement, about its often picturesque ambience, about its conquests and its results, and also about its failures and its errors. And so you could write a magnificent lesson of things, from which your successors will surely be able to draw forth the better part in the light of future struggles. In addition, if in passing you formulate certain criticisms, it will be understood that in them it is a question of advertisement or of advice that your knowledge of the facts explains and justifies. And then, does not the short history of a movement as much discussed as yours offer an interest amply sufficient interest in itself, so that you ought not to undervalue its importance?"

Language of that kind is such that it touches an author, even if he is one who is the most indifferent, the most timid, and the least sure of himself. Those are golden words that bring many temptations to write a book.

It is certain that, presented in an objective manner, aside from any personal justification, such memoirs could usefully serve the cause of Astrology. But this task appeared to be strewn with pitfalls of all sorts; would it, for example, be possible to mask the personality of the narrator sufficiently, so that these confidences could first of all assume a character of general interest?

And when I objected that it was rather in the decline of life, when it can be seen at a glance, that an author writes only the most opportune of his disclosures, they told me:

"The present war marks the end of an epoch, the end of a world. The times that will succeed it will have no resemblance to those that preceded it. Those years of conflict were a gigantic crucible in which a complete reconstitution of our ideas, of our philosophical and scientific beliefs, and of our social and political conceptions was taking place. At any rate, the period that will follow the present upheavals will not have any apparent ties with those that we have known; an impressive gulf will always separate them from one another. A narration stopping at the war or ending with it, would not be lacking in any way in its extent or completeness. On the contrary, it would end at a moment which in the history of the world would inevitably constitute a landmark, a turning-point."

After many hesitations, I ended by resorting to these arguments of apparent pertinence. It is true in any case that the renaissance movement in astrology has arrived at a dead end, from which only some new efforts, judiciously contrived, will be able to make it emerge. I have therefore passed in review those acts of which I was a witness, in order to select from among them those that could constitute for my present and future readers a useful lesson of things, a source of references or of documentation, a constant motive of encouragement, and sometimes even a guide. I have in any case striven to eliminate from these confidences everything that was not really of public interest.

If from time to time I have introduced certain personal details here, it is in order to explain certain facts better, or to permit a more exact appreciation of certain possibilities; young students in particular will find in them matter for personal meditations with regard to the conduct of their own enterprises and the allocation of their efforts. If here and there I have yielded somewhat to the pleasure of relating some amusing adventure or other among the thousands of psychological experiences that it was given to me to encounter, it is because they throw some light on the public reactions to astrology, because they are very comical, or, on the contrary, because they illustrate the moral or mental disarray into which men can fall at certain particularly grave hours of their lives. Finally, if I have often spoken about occultism in these memoirs, it is because occultism conditioned my existence, well before astrology, and at least as much as it has done.

And so, I do not have an assignment here to write the history of the astrological movement, for such an objective would be a useless repetition of the **Encyclopédie**,[2] in which my colleague and friend, the Viscount de Herbais de Thun, relates and catalogues with the ordering and minutiae that are second nature to him, everything that touches upon that movement either near or far. But perhaps it will be the case that I will add some decorations to the margins of that history, and, as a supplement to it, some ornaments that are picturesque and not without interest.

In short, here are my confidences; they embrace twenty years of astrological activity, and thirty to thirty-five years of theoretical and practical occultism.

---

2 *Encyclopédie du Mouvement astrologique de la langue française* (Brussels: *Éditions de la revue Demain*, 1944), a marvelously detailed account of those early 20th century astrologers who wrote in the French language.

Looking for a Vocation

How did I come to astrology? And why? It is all a story, the end result of a whole series of uncertainties, reboundings from circumstances, and researches about myself!

For it was in all sincerity that I entered upon the study of it, and not from any deliberate design sparked by a commercial or professional interest for example. Besides, such an interest did not exist in those heroic times, in which some rare searchers, scattered in the four corners of Belgium, represented the entire astrological movement.[3] And when I call to mind that epoch, going back over the vista of my life and the sequence of stubborn efforts that I have been obliged to make since then, I sometimes say to myself that it required a singular mélange of faith, candor, and guts to dare to undertake the organization of so thankless a movement; for it was certain that that movement would constantly run up against public indifference, and even public skepticism or hostility.

Chiefly, I would like to present myself, friend reader, under some quite ordinary appearance! No pointed hat, like the images of Épinal![4] No prestigious robe, all covered with stars, which

---

[3] Translator's Note. Astrology in Belgium, as in most of continental Europe, had died out in the 17th century, and had only begun to come back to life in the early 20th century. The revival began in France around 1890 and slowly spread to the other European countries, particularly after 1918. This is the astrological renaissance that Brahy mentioned previously.

[4] Translator's Note. The town of Épinal was the center of an industry producing cheap images, lithographs, and illustrations.

would suit so well the astrologers of the Middle Ages! I do not pose either as an "initiate," or the possessor of an unpublished "revelation"; I do not declare myself to be a "mage," or a "fakir," or even simply a "Professor," which is quite the least title to which it is necessary to pretend, it seems, if one wishes to assure himself ipso facto of the confidence and the ear of the multitude!

No! Truly! I was and I am still only a man like other men. No eccentricity, no vestments, no headgear to draw attention to me! I do not even have what is commonly called the head of an artist, nor even an unusual physiognomy! Personally, I consider myself to be an "ordinary" type, but one somewhat difficult in his tastes and appreciations, constantly musing on one idea after another. But, in the eyes of others—I know it, for I have often been told—I pass for a bizarre being, not seeing things as the world does, overturning already accepted ideas and "standard" opinions, and one who shows himself to be steadily persistent—indeed, stubborn—in the pursuit of his plans.

As for prestige, admit that there is better! My exterior appearance keeps people in reserve, indeed on the defensive; it restrains—at least at first—any burst of sympathy. How in fact can they trust someone whose reactions they can never foresee because it is always a matter of a personal mode dependent on his judgment alone? How to admit that a man built externally on the same model as others can be animated by ideals that are uncommon and often scarcely even accessible? How to understand that he does not consider each being as an indivisible unit, and that he can admire publicly, for example, the pluck of a personage under discussion, while at the same time he disapproves no less visibly of his opinions or his ideas? Or again that he does not agree with the usages or the considered opinion of everybody else, thus putting himself in some way on the outskirts of society?

That is a little like the lot of Uranians in general, especially when they are strongly impregnated with the feelings of independence and originality that the sign Aquarius emits.

Certainly, I am sometimes sorry that I lack that point of conformity—that conformity that normalizes and facilitates social relations so much. Alas! My spirit, rigorously positive and avid for truth, guards itself as if from the plague from the "sheep" of Panurge.[5] And that is why I am capable, in certain circumstances, of playing Don Quixote, of espousing unpopular causes, or of putting myself in the position of a righter of wrongs! A dangerous attitude, as it was, and the cause of numerous equivocations, but one that flows naturally from the almost morbid concern for sincerity that animates me, and which is imparted in my natal chart by the planet Saturn in the sign of Libra.

I also quite often deplore my lack of imagination and audacity! With a little "cheek"—as one says familiarly—in what a magnificent frame would I have been able to place my enterprises, and, indirectly, these memoirs! The public at large would have easily admitted—in fact, they would have found it entirely natural—that I had presented myself to them as some mysterious descendant of a maharajah, who, driven from his paternal palace by dramatic circumstances, would have been taken in by a lama or a fakir and initiated by him into the most profound mysteries of occultism! In the opinion of the masses, my prestige would have been multiplied tenfold; but by contrast, I would have lost what I have now won—the esteem of serious people who consider astrology from the exact angle that is proper to it. And I am more desirous of that than I am of the other, since I have a weakness for quality rather than for quantity.

One of my good French "confreres," having dressed himself up ridiculously for the event with a pseudonym that was entirely that of a "black mage," tried for several years to make use of it.[6] He perhaps won some naive admirers by it, but he also had a lot of diffi-

---

[5] Translator's Note. The faithful companion of Pantagruel in François Rabelais's satiric novel of the same name.

[6] Translator's Note. Probably a reference to Dom Neroman, the *enfant terrible* of French astrology in the 1930s. His pseudonym was originally spelled "Necroman", which suggests *le dom de la nécromancie* 'the lord of necromancy'.

culty in being taken seriously because of it!

Only a poet can permit himself to dress up a reality that he judges to be too imperfect! The great lyric poet that was Gabriele d'Annunzio [1863-1938] would have gladly let everyone believe that he was born, like Aphrodite, from the foam of the sea! After all, that was only one more fable for a man whose function is precisely that of making a work of the imagination, of putting a little bit of a dream, into dull reality! We merely smiled—d'Annunzio had perpetrated many other fables!—and we let him make a poem out of his life.

But should such quackery be pardoned in the case of an astrologer, a little conscious of his responsibilities and of the rigorous requirements of the science that he defends?

I easily console myself for that lack of "savoir-faire." After all, I am what my natal chart has created me, self-willed and obstinate, and I no doubt have the reputation that I deserve! It would be better not to dwell too long on this sort of thing.

"So, then, we have here a complicated being," you are going to say! "He assuredly did well to become an astrologer! It was without doubt his true vocation!"

In that, dear friend reader, you would not be deceiving yourself at all!

For my vocation as an astrologer, if it existed in germ from my adolescence, took a long time to appear! You are going to be able to judge! And it is perhaps more complicated than you would think!

Some preliminary details on my period of "incubation" will no doubt help you better to understand why. If they are too personal, I beg your pardon; a little dissection of myself will, I think, not stand in the way of the introduction to the discussion.

I was born at Liège, the first of February 1894 around 11 P.M. (birth-certificate time). If I am giving this data precisely, it is because in these "Confidences" there will be a question many times of my "horoscope." And since it has already fallen into the public domain (it was in fact published, as an example, in my book *Contribution à l'étude de l'astro-dynamique*), there exists no reason for me to conceal the details. On the contrary, the developments that I shall draw from it in passing will, I think, constitute an interesting lesson.

As far back as I can recall in my youth, I always had the impression of having lived more or less on the margin of life. Is it the fact that I was an only child that caused it? My games were solitary, and with me the exaltation of spirit took the place of the physical animation that results quite naturally from group recreations. I dream of adventures, of brilliant actions, and of epic conquests. For me, nature itself is company and a confidant. I do not have those equivocal curiosities that generally characterize the unprofitable age; my uneasinesses are more internal and tend already towards an indescribable something inaccessible and mysterious that would call to me like a lost homeland.

My father, a Government civil servant, a taciturn man, with rigid principles, and an unbelievable severity (did he not almost go to the point of disowning me one day because I had kept secret my having been kept after school?), freezes me with his distant attitude and his lack of understanding. However, proofs of his affection were not lacking; but it is an internal and reasoned affection that does not warm the heart. My mother, certainly more "humane," but required by her duties as a spouse and a private woman, and totally submissive to the marital authority, to hold back her demonstrations of tenderness almost always, and to remain before all else the punctilious educator. I grew up therefore in a sort of moral solitude, relying on myself, living in a world of my own that my meditations had constructed in its entirety.

After that, is it necessary then to be surprised that literature and poetry begin to attract me? My imagination finds a salutary outlet in lyric poetry. I write my first verses then and my first stories. A little later in high school, some of my school-fellows and myself found a periodical, in which each of our temperaments is already sketched out; one of us is melancholy, another spiritual, a third sarcastic; some are already teasing politics!

Le Falot[7]—that is the title of that periodical—permits us to flirt with the Muses alongside our studies. But already I am drawing on my nights to listen to the demon of inspiration.

Some writers have the gift of arousing my enthusiasm; d'Annunzio for example becomes one of my bedtime authors, for his lyricism opens up unsuspected profundities to me; I read and reread "The Triumph of Death," "The Fire," and "The Virgins on the Heights." But above all it is Flaubert[8] who arouses my admiration and serves as a model for me; I study his manuscripts, I follow his incessant effort for perfection through the successive versions of "Salammbô" and "Madame Bovary." I dream of becoming a novelist in my own turn.

In 1913 the French periodical *Nos loisirs* [*Our Leisures*] opens a literary competition; I participate in it with a tale of ancient inspiration "La Nuit d'Ortygie,"[9] that has the good fortune to be given first prize. At a stroke my literary vocation takes shape, and one after another I publish my first two slim volumes, **Le Poéme des Mains**,[10] a collection of poems in prose and **La Nuit d'Ortygie**, a set of short stories, that includes, in addition to the prize-winning story of which I am going to speak, two other tales: **Légende barbare** and **Toute sa Mort**.[11] Be it said in passing, I inveigh against what I call at that epoch "the rapacity" of publishers, a rapacity that appears quite moderate to me now that I have had contact with the cold realities of publishing. Alas! The war of 1914 comes to abruptly interrupt my career, and it obliges me to envisage the future in a positive fashion! This material problem comes

---

[7] Translator's Note. The word *Falot* has two meanings in French: 'lantern' and 'oddball'. Which one the young men had in mind is uncertain—perhaps both.

[8] Translator's Note. Gustave Flaubert (1821-1880).

[9] Translator's Note. "The Night of Ortygia." Ortygie is the French form of Ortygia, another name for the Greek island of Delos.

[10] Translator's Note. "The Poem of the Hands."

[11] Translator's Note. The "Barbarous Legend" and "All of his Death."

6

moreover to add to certain philosophical and religious problems that torment me for several years.

Raised in the Catholic faith, I felt myself rapidly assailed by doubts and uncertainties, and from age thirteen to eighteen I pass through the alternatives of mysticism and atheism without being able to find an equilibrium. I begin to think up one or more systems of scientific religion, in which reason would be satisfied, and the automatism of chastisements and rewards would be assured. But none of these creations eventually satisfied me! Besides, they are only child's-play, and I have a presentiment that there must exist some better crafted certitudes and revelations. The occultists assert that one who searches for the way of truth infallibly ends by finding it, and in whatever measure that he shows himself worthy of. It is too natural not to be true! An artist-painter, whose acquaintance I make at that epoch and who takes me into his friendship has me read *Les Grands Initiés* [1889] of Schuré.[12] It is the beginning of a new orientation of my philosophical concepts. Simultaneously I make contact with the ideas of Brûck.[13] Then a lady friend of my own family, divining even before I did the vocation that torments me, passes me that curious work of Lagrange that is entitled *De la Concordance qui existe entre la loi de Brück, la Chronologie de la Bible et celle de la Grande Pyramide de Chéops.*[14] Thus, there is affirmed in me the feeling, hitherto unconscious, that there exists, outside of the reach of the vulgar, a compendium of secret knowledge whose attainment presents no impossibility to a resolute man.

---

[12] Translator's Note. *The Great Initiates* of Édouard Schur (1841-1929).

[13] Translator's Note. Major Remy Brück.

[14] Translator's Note. The 2nd edition of this book by Ch. Lagrange was published by Libr. Kiesling & Cie. at Brussels in 1924.

Initiation into the Phenomena of Spiritualism

And the processes of my initiation into occultism develop in the classic manner. At some time thereafter, spiritualism opens its mysteries to me, and under circumstances that are worthy of being related.

We are in the year 1916; material necessities resulting from the war have forced me to abandon my plans for university studies and confined me in the country in an administrative post. One day, returning from an external mission, I find my clerk engaged with a singular being with a Mephistophelian physiognomy. My poor devil of an employee is pale; he is manifesting a visible effort and is clinging to the back of his chair as if he had encountered Lucifer in person. However, he benefits from my return to the office to request my permission for him to go home then. He would later confess to me to having downed two large glasses of alcohol gulp after gulp, in order to calm his emotions! In effect, there was something that would not let him feel at ease before that strange personage—who was, however, only a simple doctor of medicine—and who, having once terminated the affairs that led him to my office, has undertaken to speak to me about spiritualism and occultism! While I am forcing myself to determine whether I am dealing with a madman, with a demon, or simply with a fanatic, some words that are strange and sometimes new are striking my ear: **medium, incarnation, astral plane, clairaudience,** etc. In short, I am feeling myself disconcerted, and my visitor is taking his leave without my having been able to form any opinion with regard to him. But he has given me his address and opened his library to me. From that time, during the course of the following weeks, profiting from his authorization, I am devouring an impressive series of works treating of metapsychic phenomena. And, without taking a proper account at that moment of everything that this new stage of my initiation has of imperfection, I feel that I have taken a great step forward along the path of knowledge.

I have an opportunity then to be present for the first time at a spiritualist séance.

On a cheerful autumn afternoon, therefore, I find myself seated, along with some brave male and female companions of the neighborhood, around a big table in the modest dwelling of my previous day's visitor. The meeting begins with several minutes of meditation during which our host reads a special prayer designed to synchronize our thoughts and to distance us from those material cares that have necessarily accompanied us here. Then, each of us collects his thoughts in a sort of respectful expectation, the motive of which I cannot at first understand.

This silence, impressive enough as it is, is soon disturbed by an unexpected manifestation, which at first seemed to me to be an expression of the most purely unrestrained sort, and one that scandalized me greatly. In fact, one of those present happens to make one of those plaintive yawns that denotes either a laborious digestion or an immeasurable fatigue! And, as if that had been a signal, now many others begin to stretch and sigh grievously. Presently, I have to take into account that these are the early signs of the "phenomenon of entrancement." These manifestations diminish, however; but the wails, although they become a little less frequent, gain in intensity. And suddenly, without my having been able to record any transition whatsoever, there is a strange voice, as if in a closed vessel, speaking beside me. The woman next to me, still sunk down the instant before, sits up straight, but her physiognomy has taken on a strange and almost grievous expression. And her features are constricted stone-hard, and—what is most noticeable—her eyes appear dilated and fixed like those of a hawk.

I am taking part in the phenomenon called "incarnation." The woman next to me, who is a medium, has fallen into a trance. According to the spirit doctrine, her double has left her body, and that of a deceased person, a disincarnate, has taken its place. The "Spirit" in question, then, speaks through the mouth of its medium, and, according to the ritual that is customary in séances of this sort, the conversation begins thus:

—"Hello, my dear brothers!"

—"Hello, my dear spirit! We are happy to receive you among us! Who are you?"

The spirit that manifests itself is, it appears, the spouse of a little old woman, simple and proper, who is seated facing me, and who does not seem to be the least bit astonished by what is happening. And now it happens that, between this gracious old woman and my medium neighbor, a touching conversation takes place, just as the two spouses would have been able to do by their fireside while both were living. They recall a series of recollections of their common past; the deceased gives words of encouragement to his widow in her solitary existence, gives her some practical advice, declares that he is happy in his new situation and thanks her for the attentions given to the area surrounding his tomb. Then his voice commences to weaken; one truly feels that the force that has permitted him to manifest himself is declining; then there is the peroration:

—"Now my dear friends, I am retiring. I am happy to have been able to speak to you!"

I see my neighbor then sinking down again, then little by little returning to her senses, and rubbing her eyes, as if she were awakening from a long sleep or from a prolonged fainting spell. She moaned for some moments as if she had been beaten unmercifully; some hypnotic passes are then made over her. Soon, she completely returns to herself, but she maintains a slightly bewildered air in her state of ignorance of what really happened.

Other analogous phenomena follow. Then, abruptly, an almost tragic incident occurs: five mediums of the group are found to be simultaneously entranced by spirits who declare themselves to be those of soldiers recently killed at the front: two Germans and three French. All of them demand bugles, drums, and rifles; they are still dominated by the horrors of the combat in which they found death; they are excited, beginning to curse and threatening to come to blows. The intervention of the competent members of the group is required to deliver the mediums and to prevent their coming to blows.

This first contact with the phenomena of the beyond obviously leaves me with a curious impression—perhaps even a little deceptive—but one that has no definite character. These phenomena are certainly interesting, but too subjective in spite of everything. I have a desire to take part in some acts of more general import, or—who knows?—in a demonstration that would touch me personally.

But I remain prudent, indeed skeptical. If I should disclose myself of this desire to my doctor-Mephisto, or even to one of his co-religionaries, who would give me a guarantee, if not of the authenticity of the act itself, at least of its spontaneity? If the beyond must speak to me, I want it to be without an intermediary!

And, some days later, without my having said a word, my desire is granted!

I shall always recall that second séance to which I had been invited one morning in the vicinity of Brussels. A remarkable medium was going to be present, but they had taken care to forewarn me that it was simply a matter of a meeting of the interior order and that no experimental manifestation would take place. My interest in this séance was, in these circumstances, very minimal; nevertheless, for the sake of local color and documentation, I decided even so to attend at the stated location.

We were some twenty people there, a group seated like the first time around an immense table, which cut the room in two by its length. Chance had seated me to the left of the medium. The séance began according to the hallowed rite: meditation, prayers, appeal to the benefic forces. Then the head of the group spoke. He declared his regret at having to state that the actions of certain members were not in harmony with the moral spirit that prescribed goodness, charity, and disinterest. "It is not worthwhile to make spiritualists of you," he said, "if you must continue to let yourselves be carried away by all sorts of passions." In short, this was an admonition that would not have been out of place at a Christian love-feast of the early ages, and one whose sincerity shone forth so much the more because it was addressed to simple souls.

The head of the group cited some specific actions, publicly accused one of the members present, and appealed to his good resolutions, and to his repentance. He pointed out the baseness of the act that he had committed (it was a matter of an abortion), and he finished by making an appeal to the prayers and good thoughts of all those present, so that the stray sheep might rapidly find again the way to the sheepfold.[15]

It was at that moment that the unexpected launched itself!

For some moments, the medium at my right had been giving some manifest signs of agitation. The friend who had accompanied her, recognizing the signs preceding a trance, proposed to let the events come. The chief had an opposite opinion: "Today we have a séance devoted solely to moralization," he said, "therefore, there is no place for phenomena that would be foreign to the end pursued!"

To this, his interlocutor retorted that perhaps the spirits had a communication to make, and that, in any case, it would do more harm to the medium to thwart the trance than to let it be produced freely.

As well as we could see, the moment after that, my neighbor

---

[15]I was largely inspired by these actions to write my play in three acts, "Un Drame chez les Spirites" [A Drama Among the Spirits].

collapsed in her chair, as empty of substance, only to sit up straight again, somewhat mechanically. And her face took on the haggard and congealed expression that I had already remarked at the time of my first contact with this kind of phenomenon.

She surveyed the assembly slowly with that empty look, which is the essential characteristic of one who has been possessed; and suddenly we heard a serious voice emanate from her mouth, while she simulates the act of washing her hands, as if to rid herself of undesirable fluids:

—"There is something of violet here; violet is the color of evil!"[16]

Then the entity gave a veritable sermon, tinged, like that given by the head of the group, with the purest morality, but which had a still more penetrating accent, more dramatic, more dangerous even. It attacked some other imperfections noted among other members; it ended with an exhortation to do better, encouraging each one to behave well, in spite of the difficulties and the sorrows due to the war. And, with that remark, it inquired whether anyone of those present had a desire to express, for example a desire to obtain news of some being from whom they were momentarily separated.

The mother of a family who for a long time had not received any letters from her two sons, exiles in Germany, expressed the uneasiness that she held. After a short moment, the spirit replied to her:

—"I see your two children doing agricultural work, they are in good health. So do not be uneasy! The news that you are waiting for has been delayed in route, and it will reach you soon. It will confirm what I am going to say to you."[17]

No other question having been formulated, the spirit had begun to pronounce the words:

---

[16] Such an affirmation will seem strange to certain of my readers, for it contradicts certain occult teachings. I only repeat what I heard.

[17] These details were in fact confirmed by the receipt of a letter that arrived several days later.

14

—"Now, my friends, I am retiring . . ."

when it stopped short, seeming to fix on the presence of something invisible for assistance. Then it asked again:

—"I see here a very small soul . . . it seems to be searching for someone . . . it is the soul of a person who has died suddenly . . . Has anyone in the room lost a member of his family that way?"

I felt myself seized at that moment with a poignant emotion, for I was thinking about the desire that I had formulated for myself a few days earlier . . . my mother had in fact died unexpectedly of an embolism three years previously.

The spirit added:

—"It is a lady, she is a little timid, she is looking for someone here; after her death, they tied a handkerchief around her chin."

These words made me recall a detail of the funereal dressing of my mother; as often happens in such a case, they had adjusted a band around her head to immobilize her lower jaw. This detail was assuredly a petty one; however, I had at that moment an absolute presentiment that my mother was there, present, and wanted to speak to me. But, my skepticism taking the upper hand, I succeeded in containing my emotion and preserving an impenetrable countenance.

The medium, during this time, seeing that no one was following up her question, placed her glassy gaze successively on each one of those present. I see her again now, her eyes strangely fixed, turning themselves like a robot towards the person situated on her right, passing thus from one to the other, to arrive at scrutinizing my neighbors seated at the end of the table where I was placed, and, finally, stopping her gaze on me:

—"But have you not had this case in your family? Did your mother not die suddenly?"

At the height of emotion, I had to confess to the fact, and then the spirit said to me:

—"Well, it is your mother that is here, my child! See, she is coming towards you, she bends over, she embraces you! (And her gaze, always fixed and in some way hypnotic, seemed to follow across the space that a person of medium height would occupy, a person who would stop near me, and then bend over towards me!) Unhappily, she could not manifest herself directly; she was already too evolved, too far from the earth for that! So that she could only communicate with me, so that I am repeating to you what she would have wished to say to you! She caught your thought several days ago, and she has wanted to assure you herself of her constant presence near you. During her life, certain misunderstandings occurred between the two of you; the affection that you both bore for each other was not always manifested as you would have liked. But now it is necessary to live with the remembrance of your mother as if she were still here at your side. You must put her portrait near you, speak to her, explain your difficulties and your doubts to her, and you will see, you will feel her presence then, and she will often serve you well as a guide."

The spirit said to me again that my mother was profoundly catholic, that after her death she had looked for paradise—which she believed she had merited by her pious life—but that she had not found it, and that for that reason she felt very disoriented. It revealed to me certain intimate or familial details that I alone had the power to know, or even that I was totally ignorant of, and whose exactitude I was later able to verify. Then it requested me again to think of my mother, to consider her as always living near me.

—"Now, she says goodbye to you," it said. "She embraces you again!"

And, before leaving the trance, it seemed to follow with its eyes fixed the progress of a shade that went across the room.

It is superfluous to say that this séance had profoundly upset me, not only from all that which it implied for a subjective proof, but especially by its spontaneity and the unforeseen occurrence that had presided there and which constituted for me an argument of a value superior even to the demonstration itself.

As for the rest, I was able to be present, in this group and in others, at multiple manifestations of what is called "spirit phenomena": blows, knocks, table turnings, conversations by means of the planchette (or, Ouija), automatic writing, clairvoyance, clairaudience, mummification of living matter, dividing in two, etc. And that gave me the conviction—for the moment, at least—that the spirit theory—which preaches the reincarnation of souls and the fated payment of injustices and bad actions—was the scientific religion that I had for a long time been searching for. Besides, did it not carry along in its train—notably, in the sect of the Antoinists[18]—a vagueness of sincerity and mysticism like that which animated the Christians in the time of the Roman persecutions? Did they not see, a little on all sides, spirits healing maladies without asking for any remuneration from that principal; and their improvised temples accepting with the same fervor, and in the same simplicity, the rich as well as the poor? Suddenly, I recovered my philosophical equilibrium. Possessed by the thirst for a perfect religion, I was moving automatically towards the summit of the doctrine without lingering in the thousand enigmas, contradictions, and dangers of the experimental practice. It was not the dead or their simulacra that I was asking to guide me on the way filled with shadow, on which I was going to set out, it was Truth itself, unique, always present everywhere, and which delivers one or another of its facets simply according as one contemplates it from one angle of view or another.

---

[18] Translator's Note. A minor Christian sect formed according to some sources by a Belgian, Louis Antoine, in the 1890s and reported to have had 100,000 members in 1900. It was a mixture of Christianity and spiritualism.

First Contacts with Magic and the Science of the Stars

Meanwhile, the war coming to an end, life was reorganizing itself little by little. International exchanges resumed; the currents of ideas began to be interchanged again from one nation to another. I remained tortured by the thirst for knowledge, and, in the midst of the material cares that very unfortunately assailed me at that time, I clung to my hope of pursuing the study of the Great Mystery.

But before [I could do that] I had to surmount two serious handicaps. On the one hand, I was going to get married, and from that time on a truly extraordinary [siege of] bad luck pursued me; at no other time of my life—save perhaps at the end of the Second World War—have I suffered the same number of injustices, of disappointments and misunderstandings, that one would have said were expressly created to annihilate and baffle my efforts! I had resigned from the Administration, in which, however, I would have been able to carve out a very nice future; but everything that I had been able to observe there during the German occupation—illegal favors, favoritism, negligence, scandals, petty hypocrisies and surrenders of principle of all kinds had disgusted me as much as if I had been a victim of it directly. I felt myself becoming an anarchist. The army had then recalled me, and the necessity of remaking a position for myself fell upon me urgently.

Besides, the famous Spanish Influenza of 1919 had made me very ill, and, finally, terribly weakened; I was not dead from it but not much better than dead. Attended by an incompetent military doctor, I had not been able to get well, and, on top of that—in order to avoid losing an opportune position—I had, after my demobilization, taken up my new duties without taking the convalescent leave which would have been indispensable to me in the state of exhaustion in which I found myself. This turned out to be a grave error that I am still paying for today. In effect, all intellectual work had become extraordinarily difficult for me; a kind of encephalitis was literally dulling my mind, and, at certain moments, reasoning became entirely impossible for me. I have spent long years in recuperation, but still my memory has remained very deficient—so much so that it was a great handicap for me later when I took up astrology.

As much good as bad, drawing still on my already insufficient dream, to the point of continually compromising my recovery—which shows that I was obedient to a simple passion, a mental passion instead of a physical one, that was the sole difference!—however, I succeeded in continuing my studies of occultism. One of my friends, pressed for money, had to sell a good part of his library; I had bought it from him, and thus I fell into possession of numerous works treating of astrology and magic.

At first, magic monopolized my curiosity. At a stroke, those vast horizons that spiritualism had opened up to me found themselves surpassed. An almost infinite succession of perspectives opened up in their stead, and I was not without experiencing some vertigo from always advancing thus, without end, to mount ceaselessly into the whole sky, to see assembling under my own eyes the elements of a formidable and redoubtable synthesis. For it revealed itself as something so different from everything that I had supposed, so superior to everything that I had dreamed of, that it was forcibly making me into a being apart, who could never anymore see and judge things like a common mortal.

That study, however, was not going along without danger! A

singularly balanced mental organization is necessary to engage in occultism! How many searchers of my sort have been victims of it and have sunk lugubriously into obsession, mental derangement, indeed into madness! One day, however, I had a singular experience! I was plunged deeply into reading some work or other on magic; and, once again, my mental horizons had just been strangely enlarged. It was then that I felt very clearly the impression that a sort of physical vertigo was seizing me, that a kind of cold breath—clearly perceptible—was overwhelming me, and that I was literally out of my depth! Fortunately, the instinct of self-preservation made me react almost automatically! In an instant I had closed the book and replaced it in my bookcase, taking the precaution even of removing the key to the bookcase.

That state of vertigo lasted for eight days, during which time I was able to meditate and interrogate myself at my leisure on what had happened to me. Later, I realized that I had then undergone my first effective contact with what is called the "astral plane," the "Guardian of the Threshold." That experience, a little moving at first, is nevertheless one of the most benign of all those that it is necessary to confront when one wishes to conquer the Invisible.

One would not know how to repeat often enough that the practice of occultism, and particularly magic should not be entered upon without the assistance or the supervision of a qualified Master. Because he wanted to gratify his dangerous curiosity by evoking the forces of the Invisible, one of my friends has remained dangerously possessed and has been a victim of truly dramatic circumstances.

As for myself, since I had practiced some respiratory yoga exercises for several months, I had effectively developed a sort of second sight or a faculty of dividing myself in two that put me into contact with the inhabitants of another world. Thus, when I awoke at night, I would see something like white phantoms at the foot of my bed; but these visions were perfectly peaceful and of a reassuring, indeed of an agreeable, aspect. A strange declaration, but a classic one; when I would try to discern their lineaments or to penetrate into their intentions, these subtle forms invariably vanished. But the counterpart of that commencement of clairvoyance was the creation of a sort of divorce or "dislocation" between my physical envelope and my invisible bodies. The result of this was a state of somnambulism translating itself into nightmares or daydreams, during which I was doing something and moving about unconsciously. How many times has it happened that I recovered my spirits outside of my room or while turning the light switch? And sometimes long moments would pass before I completely recovered my lucidity of thought.

Also, one will understand that, made somewhat uneasy by these unwonted manifestations, which also frightened my wife terribly, I shut myself up in an attitude of expectation until the day when I could resume my occult training in the light of qualified counsels.

At the mercy of circumstances, however, my experimental knowledge continually grew more extensive. I had an opportunity on rare occasions to take part in experiments involving hypnotism, auto-suggestion, and especially the release of the sensibilities—experiments analogous to those that were conducted methodically by Col. Albert de Rochas. These experiments, entirely curious, indeed astonishing, explain and bring in the phenomenon of spell-making, that demoniac practice that many people consider to be a superstition, a silly whiff of the naïve Middle Ages. But the experiments in which I took part naturally made me see quite well that the phenomenon is real, or at least that it can become so.

But, as that had already been produced with spiritualism, the practical side of magic (or the "spectacular side," if I can call it that) rapidly lost its attractions in my eyes. I had understood that the "curiosity" element, dilettantism, and amateurism constituted precisely the greatest danger of occultism, the most subtle temptation, and the one most imminent to surmount. I was obliged to admit that the surest key to Hermetism was disinterest, the desire to serve and to make oneself useful. Nothing is more certain than that this attitude—which could pass for heroism or sacrifice in the eyes of certain individuals, preoccupied essentially with material enjoyments—is difficult to maintain in present-day life. However, for me it did not present any difficulty in adhering to it, and so I progressively detached myself from many illusions and false needs engendered by the cult of appearances, of conformism, and fleeting things. Saturn, the planet of renunciation, predominant in my natal horoscope, and Venus its ruler, placed in the sign Pisces, the natural sign of sacrifice, presided quite naturally over the necessary moral condition.

Since that time, Hermetism, properly said, with its abstraction and its symbols, has occupied me a good bit more than occultism itself.

—And astrology? What became of it in all that, you might ask me.

Patience! We are coming to it!

Until then, it had only interested me as a purely documentary item; I considered it simply as a chapter in the ensemble of occult sciences, such as physiognomy, chiromancy, and graphology; and I had studied it in that manner, but without making it the object of any real specialization. What intrigued me, however, was to learn whether the planetary influences mentioned in these diverse sciences represented anything real. There too, I was looking for a proof, a serious indicator that would induce me to get to the bottom of the matter.

Now, when I was glancing through a manual giving a description of the various planetary influences, it quite often happened that I would recognize certain traits of my own character in the solar, Mercurian, or Jupiterian influences; but, on reading the descriptions devoted to Venus, Mars, or Saturn, I would also recognize in them certain other characteristics of my temperament. This constant state of uncertainty and hesitation discouraged me and ended by becoming an irritant.

I had certainly heard about certain practitioners, notably Mr. De Landtsheer, the doyen of Belgian astrologers; but he, it was said to me, was living in a sort of ivory tower, and besides, his professional duties left him little leisure time. I judged then that it would be nearly useless to make an attempt along that line—is it pride? is it timidity?—I have always hated to disturb other people or to solicit something from them. On the contrary, I prefer to receive advances from others, which puts me very much more at ease.

Happily, chance came once more to my aid! I happened one day to stop in front of an announcement of a lecture on astrology. Naturally, I did not fail to go there. Lost in the heart of a sizable crowd, I was present at some very convincing demonstrations, the predictions made by the speaker having been recognized by those interested as corresponding to some precise events.

The speaker, although taking refuge behind a pseudonym, was congenial and seemed to be graciously affable. Therefore, I did not have much to restrain me from asking him at the end of the session the question that was burning on my lips: "Do you make horoscopes?"

To my great surprise, his reply was evasive! He promised to write to me. In fact, he did write to me, but he continued to conceal his identity and surrounded all his correspondence with circumstances that were at once mysterious and rather romantic. Was it a bluff? I don't know; at least that was not his essential motive! Perhaps my interlocutor simply wanted to give more weight to his revelations through the allurement of mystery. Still, it was only after several weeks of impatience that I received a study of my natal horoscope. To my great surprise, the study said:

"You were born under the influence of Saturn, which makes saints and rebels!"

Under the influence of Saturn! The planet malefic par excellence! I had considerable difficulty at first in accepting that verdict!

But then, aided by reflection, I took into account, in effect, that the basis of my character was indeed that of a mystic, an independ ent, a stubborn person, and a "plodder," hard on himself and strongly attached to principles, and, moreover, one on whom life had not hitherto showered its favors. And I concluded that all those other influences that I believed to have recognized in myself were merely accessories. I thought then of certain friends, whose existence was easier or happier than mine; if Venus or Jupiter, the most propitious planets, had been obliged to play a principal role in my horoscope, what still more benefic influences would have been required to intervene in their horoscopes to justify a lot as favorable as theirs?

And, conquered by that logic, I resigned myself to accepting the verisimilitude of that Saturnian influence. Besides, I certainly had the Saturnian physique—slim stature, and a little bent over, a grave exterior, indeed a tortured appearance, a thin face, eyes sunk deep in their sockets, nose long and aquiline, complexion rather pale. And as for the rest of my influences, we shall see!

But this was like a new kind of initiation that was going to pounce upon me with a burden of responsibilities, apprehensions, and hopes without limits that every revelation allows!

An Astrological Vocation

For now the desire had been implanted in me to learn how to cast a natal horoscope and interpret it myself!

Step by step, I had been put into contact with many researchers who would already have been able, at that moment, to impart their experience with astrological science to me. That would have been a small matter—some leisure moments, some eclectic counsels. For I did not know what book to begin with, nor how to make a choice of authors, nor where to find a complete explanation of the doctrine!

First of all, the little manuals of Alan Leo had been recommended to me; they had been translated into French and were in a very practical format, since one could easily slip them into his pocket and thus have them constantly at hand's reach; that was a big advantage for me, because, having little leisure time at my disposal, I could easily consult them during my rides on the street-car. Max Heindel's *Astrology Simplified* was also favorably mentioned to me, but that book gave me a lot of trouble, since it was intended for Americans and not for Europeans; I thus had to surmount some associated difficulties—but ones that turned out to be more profitable for my initiation into astrology. I also studied *The Message of the Stars* by the same author; then the works of Alan Leo in their original language: *How to judge a Nativity*, *The Key to your own Nativity*, the *Art of Synthesis*, and *The Progressed Horoscope*.

And then I began to have my first experiences—first, with myself, then with the members of my family, and with my associates. The most immediate result was to settle me rapidly on the direction of my proper destiny. And many things were explained that had previously perplexed me.

Saturn, rising on the eastern horizon in my natal horoscope, under an unfavorable angle from Neptune, was a perfect explanation of the isolation and atmosphere of incomprehension that had constantly thrown their shadow on my life, the lack of intimacy and affection, which had always grieved me. The sign of Libra, where Saturn is placed, and the influence of Venus, the ruler of that sign occupying the sign Pisces, should otherwise have given me a very lively sensibility with an artistic and poetic disposition, a nature that was more or less chivalrous and mystical, with a spirit of sacrifice and resignation. The presence of the Sun and Mercury in Aquarius, in major aspect with Uranus and Neptune, explained at last my disdain for the conventional, my spirit of innovation and independence—indeed, of rebellion—but also my feelings for cooperation, my desire to understand the basis of things, and a certain delicacy of emotions and thoughts. These latter configurations seemed to open wide for me the access to superior worlds, but only after many proofs, which therefore demanded from me an untiring persistence. It was there, in its entirety, the horoscope of a sort of contemplative monk, still insufficiently freed from worldly affections, and in whom a Moon-Mars conjunction in the sign Sagittarius introduced a note of ardent proselytism. And that recalled to me that some years earlier, a prelate, with whom I had had many exchanges of philosophical views, had said to me, by way of conclusion: "You would have made an excellent Redemptorist!" Who knows? While remaining entirely on the lay plain, it is a fact that I do exteriorize a little of that mystic enthusiasm that must animate the true representatives of the priesthood.

To return to my "horoscope," when the Sun, progressing in my chart, had simultaneously passed a malefic aspect to Saturn and Neptune, a very difficult period should inevitably have followed for me, a period that was dangerous even, bringing disappointments, inconveniences, and even the danger of death. But in fact, it was at that epoch around 1921—and anyone studying my chart will be able to verify it in a few moments—that they launched themselves almost simultaneously, and that time of material misfortune which I have already mentioned, and that infectious influenza, which failed to lead me to a knowledge of the beyond in a manner that was certainly not one that particularly interested me.

One thing more that the study of my chart taught me, was that things of the heart would always bring me many disappointments and romantic incidents. On the one hand, the Moon in bad aspect to Uranus, and on the other hand Venus well placed by sign but retrograde and making a bad aspect to Neptune, showed that in order to have dreamed of any exceptional destiny in the realm of feelings, I would have had to hold my aspirations continually in check. Happily, marriage, without bringing any particular element of harmony, showed itself sufficiently able to channelize my sentimentality, but in a manner that was reasonable, "bourgeois," and measured—three elements that one will agree had little in harmony with what one has seen of my temperament, and in a word were placed in diametrical opposition to it.

However, aided by my youth and illusions, I did not have any faith in that warning. But now that with the vantage point of age I can judge things more sanely, I have the impression of having been like a bird in a cage, which, unaware of its situation, would not have ceased to bruise itself against the bars in the hope of taking its flight out into the open.

But I only speak of that in order to show the exactness of astrology and the little attention that one is tempted to pay to it when one is personally involved. It is difficult to be objective vis-à-vis oneself; everyone imagines that he can always overturn, by the force of his will or by his own inertia, the barriers that destiny has raised on the path of his ambitions or his desires. How many times afterwards have I been able to see young people do the same, taking no account of my warnings, and coming back to see me several years later to confess their errors!

But, while I was liberating myself from these first practical speculations, my initiation proceeded rapidly. Taking some advice from one person, participating in some talks with another, I sensed that there was forming in me a kind of special sense that I would call the astrological sense. I would have been able to learn by heart the analytical texts in the manuals, I would have been able to study the theory in the manner of a parrot; but I realized that that primary method would lead me nowhere, because it would never encompass the breadth and the infinity of possible cases. On the contrary, I had the ambition to create a synthetic system which could adapt itself to all eventualities and to all difficulties. In order to accomplish this, it would be necessary to study the symbolism of the celestial influences to the greatest extent possible.

That was what I did, decomposing the planetary hieroglyphs into their constituent parts and drawing from their juxtaposition those elements that essentially differentiated them. I worked in the same way with the signs of the Zodiac, although that had already shown itself to be more difficult. Finally, I tried to apply the same system to the divisions of the astrological chart that are called "houses," and which are in fact only a terrestrial replica of the twelve signs of the celestial Zodiac. I finished by having decomposed and dissected the astrological tradition into sufficiently restricted "detached pieces," into a kind of set of keys, or of permutations and aggregations, which permitted an infinite number of combinations. The entire science of astrology—at least, as far as the general interpretation of the chart—was enclosed therein under that set of symbols, just as the science of the Tarot is condensed into 22 plates or arcanas. And thus, having mastered almost entirely alone, the purely technical part of the study of astrology, I had the impression that I would soon be able to pass on to the exercise of application and virtuosity. I longed to hear the instrument that I had thus fabricated emit some sounds; I burned with impatience to try out its suppleness, its extent and exactitude!

But, above all that, I had a presentiment of a higher ambition in myself, that of sharing the faith that now entirely possessed me, that of burning passionately on the altar of truth, that that altar must one day change into a pyre!

Yes, I had within me an obscure need to create, to participate in the battle of ideas! My Moon-Mars conjunction in the "house" of education and in the sign of the higher sciences was making some fiery impulses of proselytism rise up in me, whereas the influence of the signs of Aquarius and Pisces incited me on the one hand to dispense freely the fruits of my own cultivation, and on the other hand to envisage the regeneration of a world mentally depraved and morally impoverished. That was the beginning of a vocation that would introduce into my life some very curious experiences and some very strange episodes.

Campaign for the Rehabilitation of a Repudiated Mother

As I have said, I am naturally timid; but even so, hunger sometimes renders even the most peaceful beings ferocious. And so on occasion the ardor of my convictions arouses in me an activity and an unsuspected boldness.

I would have been happy to follow one or the other of my predecessors if he himself had undertaken to join into a block the scattered fragments of the Belgian astrological movement; I would have felt driven to try myself to realize that unity in the right of its absence. And besides, I did not judge myself to be the one most qualified to play that role, nor the one possessing sufficient rights towards that end.

I have, in fact, already spoken of Mr. De Landtsheer, who was unanimously considered to be the doyen of Belgian astrologers; Mr. Strymans of Antwerp would perhaps have been able to lay claim to that same title; at Brussels I had received some useful advice from Mr. Chapellier and Mr. Nicolay, as well as from Albert Jorwitz. Their right to take the lead, therefore, came before mine.

But none of them demonstrated any intention of organizing a Belgian astrological movement. In the hope of galvanizing them, of inspiring in them, if not the faith that moves mountains, at least the necessary spirit of determination, I expressed to them my astonishment at seeing a situation prolonged that was so anarchical and so absolutely prejudicial to the cause of astrology. Alas! I ran into, if not incomprehension, at least hesitation and evasion! I was literally enraged that my intentions should have remained misunderstood, and that my good will was at that point so little appreciated that it found no opportunity to exert itself, even in the background. Little by little, I felt growing within me the desire to act alone and to take some definite action that would bring each one of them face-to-face with his responsibilities and would provide the maximum stimulation to their faculties of enterprise and cooperation.

What I am going to say should not be considered as a criticism directed against my predecessors and still less as blame. For, to be just, it must be admitted that the unification of the Belgian astrological movement was a serious enterprise that, in order to be properly conducted, necessarily demanded a sustained expenditure both of time and of money. Absorbed in their professional occupations, or content with more limited and more modest realizations, those I spoke to railed against my ambitious projects. And it was for that reason that, after having made some new attempts as fruitless as the earlier ones, I launched an appeal for the creation of a Belgian Astrological Institute.

It was evident that taking this step did not go without provoking some ripples in the stream—ripples that were, however, superficial and that did not depart from the plane of amity—but these ripples would infallibly dash themselves against my solid argument: "You have not tried, you who have titles greater than mine, to do any constructive work! Too bad! I am seizing the reins myself, but I am ready to hand them over at any moment to anyone who would like to take back the initiative himself."

Now, to my great astonishment, and perhaps to the astonishment of everyone, a considerable number of persons joined! Some of them were of a purely moral order, but so precious nevertheless; the others constituted some offers of real collaboration, made in a spirit of sincerity and impartiality. So that, on the 30th of May 1926, when the inaugural assembly took place, more than twenty-five people found themselves assembled with the well understood intention of forming the basis of an Astrological Institute, with a view to diffusing the science of astral influences throughout Belgium and of organizing an adequate system of instruction towards that end. A Brussels lawyer had, on his own initiative prepared some legal documents giving to the organization in question the proper legal form of a non-profit organization; he presented them to the assembly, and it approved them unanimously, being very happy to ratify a remarkable work and one that permitted the economy of numerous discussions. Mr. Jean Delville, an artist-painter and a member of the Belgian Royal Academy was pleased to accept the honorary presidency of the new Institute. The senior members of the group, Messers De Landtsheer, A. Strymans, T. Chapellier, M. Nicolay, A. Jorwitz, and many others too, brought to the new organization an affiliation as complete as their means permitted. In short, it was a memorable session! The officers were as follows:

> President (Honorary): Jean Delville
> Directors: O. De Landtsheer, Th. Chapellier, and General Buisset
> Secretary: Miss Van der Linde (later, Mrs. Th. Chapellier)
> I myself was elected Executive Secretary.

That date of 30 May 1926 marked the beginning of a new period for me, a real turning-point in my life. My Sun by progression was then exactly in a triangular (120°) aspect of Uranus, the planet of the new, the occult, the original, of bold and original beginnings, discoveries, technical progress, and of astrology itself! The Sun was forming this aspect in the 5th house of my horoscope, which is the house of creations of every kind, and consequently also of children. Is it necessary, then, to be surprised that that year 1926 was marked for me by the birth of a daughter! And that in that same year—I will speak of it at more length further on—I should have entered into the experimental domain of occultism.

One sees that everything holds in our science; and what one at first takes to be coincidences is justified and explained remarkably upon examination.

The Astrological Institute of Belgium rapidly entered the road to practical realizations. A communiqué announcing its foundation was immediately sent to the press. Some papers gave it a good welcome. Others, on the contrary, laughed and made fun of our initiative. Thus, a provincial newspaper published the following note:

> An astrological institute has been founded in our country. It will hold its opening session . . . Many newspapers have accepted the official communication of the new institute without smiling . . . **That is our position on it!**

Whereas two Brussels dailies, under different signatures, gravely printed the same text, as follows:

> The Belgian astrologers are restraining themselves! Before all else, they want to proceed scientifically and to accept nothing that is not certain. They are bringing to these studies the qualities of good sense, slowness, and moderation, by which the citizens of our nation are recognized throughout the world. Think that they count in the bosom of their association, without any goal of remuneration, an artist-painter, a retired general, a professor of music, a CPA, and some other luminaries who shine with a brighter luster in the sky of Brusselian thought. One can rely upon an Institute and upon a periodical governed by such conditions.

One can see that in the eyes of some we were passing—as was normal enough at that epoch!—for gentle illuminates, nitwits, and poor fools who were not very malicious, but whose manias were denounced!

But we were very determined, persuaded that we were doing the right thing to endure the irony of our detractors! The best way to triumph in this matter was to win public opinion—at least, the serious ones—and, if possible, the scientific world. Assuredly, the task in prospect was a long, drawn-out one, but that was not a fact to rebuff me! The natives of Liège are in fact known to be hard-headed; they have proven it throughout the course of their history! I was determined not to give the lie to my native city's reputation!

God knows, however, if the occasions of discouragement turned out to be frequent! A high official in the Finance Ministry, who had had wind of my initiative, said to me one day, paternally: "What you want to do, my dear Sir, is of course very fine, very commendable! But believe in my own experience, Belgium is a backward country, without culture, without any imagination. You are not in Holland, in Germany, or in Switzerland here! Believe me! You are going to wear yourself out in a struggle that will gain you nothing!"

That was the opinion of a person favorably disposed in regard to astrology! What can we say of the opinions that emanated from those of set purpose, from those who were jealous, or from declared adversaries! If it had been necessary to prick up one's ears to that, we would have scratched the project before entering the lists!

On the contrary, we resolved to strike a great blow! In the first session, which was public but also official, I tried to give an inventory of the reasons that underpinned my belief in astral influences. But, the Institute, shortly before holding an official session with a view to formally stating its program, invited Major Paul Choisnard, the restorer of scientific Astrology in France, to lend us his support by coming on that day to give a lecture, which, in view of the personality of the speaker, would certainly make a great noise. Paul Choisnard, always ready to serve that cause to which he had so long been devoted, agreed to make the long journey from Saintonges in Gironde to Brussels. His talk, given on 5 November 1926, at the Union Coloniale, attracted an elite public; it had a great success, and it found some sympathetic echoes in the capitol press. Paul Choisnard set forth in it the scientific astrological problem, from the angle that was very dear to him, that of statistics and probabilities. His remarks drew the attention of some who were indifferent and some skeptics. We had the pleasure of being able to reproduce them in extenso in the *Revue belge d'Astrologie moderne* [Belgian Review of Modern Astrology], the modest quarterly that we had just started at the end of 1926, to serve as the mouthpiece of the Institute, and which published the details of meetings, the titles of projected talks, the names of members and donors of the Institute, and all interesting news items concerning Astrology. Mr. De Landtsheer had already in the first issue set forth the rudiments of a course, and one also found there the announcement of his forthcoming book, *Comment dresser votre horoscope* [How to Cast Your Horoscope]. In the meantime, an embryonic library was established, Paul Choisnard having given the Institute a complete collection of his own works. One can see that we had the sacred fire and the dynamism of our persevering action leading in a short time to tangible and encouraging results. In a few months, opinion had been alerted, and the problem of astral influence categorically posed.

Mr. De Landtsheer had also put into execution his project of giving weekly course lectures, lectures that were attended by a fervent and sympathetic public. In addition, the Institute was also going to begin a series of monthly meetings designed to demonstrate the practical applications of Astrology. Mr. De Lantdsheer, General Buisset, Mr. Chapellier and myself successively developed in it various subjects of a general or technical order.

Thus, in this intellectual "adventure" that constituted the foundation of the **Institut astrologique**, we had made a good start that embodied all our hopes, and that would perhaps lead one day to the rehabilitation of that science that has so justly been named "the mother of Astronomy"—a mother abandoned, as it were!

We were also able to record certain successes of an official or semi-official order. That was the case when the aviators Medaets and Verhaegen made known their project of a long-distance flight to the Congo;[19] we offered our services to the competent authorities. They, to our great surprise, invited us to send all our useful information. It was a first result!

However, certain unexpected difficulties soon came to make us understand that it was not sufficient to give proof of good intentions to rally opinion, even that of informed circles.

The philosophical independence that had been established as the foundation of the Institute's program was going to arouse some rumblings of opposition and some unfortunate misunderstandings.

Without taking into account that certain jealousies, which, since they wore the mask of apparent good intentions, were thereby better disguised, must fatally accentuate divergences of viewpoint and create a climate that was absolutely contrary to a good mutual understanding.

---

[19] Translator's Note. This was evidently in 1927, prior to the flight in which the aviators were critically injured when their plane crashed on the Langres Plateau in France in November 1927.

About the "Commercialization" of Astrology

The talks given by the **Institut astrologique**, which were, at the beginning, given in a spacious hall on the rue de la Loi—graciously put at our disposal by Mr. Chapellier's brother—continued, when that location was no longer available, in the hall of the **Belgian Theosophical Society**, which a goodly number of our members belonged to. Perhaps that was a mistake, for our attitude of philosophical independence could have been shaken by this, nor would this have been only an appearance. The difficulty in this sort of thing is that it is not always easy to find a meeting place—one is too central, another too bothersome, and a third inadequate. Consequently, it is necessary to make a compromise among the practical possibilities. And once again one sees that only financial independence can ensure moral independence!

Meanwhile, the contact with the milieu of the Belgian Astrological Society had only reinforced my interest in occultism in general. It must be said in this regard that the founders of the Theosophical Society, Madame Blavatsky with her *Secret Doctrine* and her *Isis Unveiled*, Annie Besant and C.W. Leadbeater with *The Ancient Wisdom, The Visible and Invisible Man, Man and his Bodies, The Astral Plane, Occult Chemistry*, etc., had enlarged my conceptions anew, to the same degree that the study of spiritualism had broadened them as compared to the narrow conceptions of my youth. Was everything exact in these "revelations," made by the faking of pretended faculties of clairvoyance? It was very difficult to judge! Was it not reasonable, however, to have confidence in these authors, despite the more or less troublesome noises that accompanied their subject, and that prevented the skeptics from having faith in the mission that these founders had referred to. They deserved a profound recognition, certainly for the documentary value of their works. Even making allowance for some of the exaggerations and the possible inexactitudes, their writings brought to the occult movement some teachings that were logical, concordant, and inestimable. Besides, it is always necessary to judge things by their spirit and not by their appearances; and the fact that Blavatsky sometimes gave proof of vulgarity and was suspected of fraud, that Leadbeater had to undergo a severe condemnation, and that Annie Besant defended Malthusianism, does not in any way diminish the qualities of these investigators, nor indeed their reputation. Whoever has touched occultism, even in a small way, has in fact learned by experience how important it is to remain prudent with regard to the matter of judgments of this sort. The fact is that occultists see things from an angle that is only rarely the same as that from which common mortals see them; hence, they are more frequently subject to slander and to criticism, and the verdicts that are passed upon them are not always deserved. Besides, the public has a tendency to consider them to be like gods, forgetting that first of all they are human beings. I was then making my own the Theosophical Society's ideal of fraternity, and being desirous of applying it to the fullest extent possible, I had begun in 1926 what it is convenient to call "occult training", that is to say the development of the voluntary faculties as well as some of the psychic powers that are potentially present in the human being. In short, it was an application of the laws of magic, not to others, but to one's own self. One can scarcely press one's faith further than that!

How was it possible to determine among the adepts of theosophy some different degrees in the force of conviction, the value of the apostolate, the naïveté or the skepticism, that goes with it! Certain ones demonstrated a truly touching devotion; other took special interest in intellectual speculation, paying only a relative attention to the precepts of fraternity that had been preached to them; others believed themselves to be favored by visions or protections of an occult order; one even encountered some who clearly brushed upon a nervous or cerebral derangement and recalled the strong pronouncement of Pascal: "Who would make an angel, makes a beast!" But altogether they created an interesting ambiance, rich with good will, in which one found a permanent moral comfort and ample intellectual satisfactions. Astrology—and this astonished me—was not held in honor among them! It was tolerated, no doubt out of respect for the freedom of opinion, and because the leaders of the Theosophical movement honored it highly in their writings, but, in the gamut of the so-called occult sciences, it certainly did not obtain the place that its importance deserved. And it even seems that those who were directing the Belgian Theosophical Society at that time felt a certain satisfaction when one day they announced to me that they could no longer place their hall at the disposition of the Institute. They declared in support of their decision that I was orienting myself to the "commercialization" of Astrology. I don't want to reply here to that accusation; I will return to it later, for it deserves to have an ample refutation.

This verdict was always conveyed to me in a solemn manner at the end of a meeting of the Administrative Council of the Theosophical Society. Its terms had been seriously discussed.

Was the motive invoked sincere? Or was it concealing some spite? Let us not linger to answer the question. However, it must be known that when the Astrological Institute was founded, certain theosophists had believed that it was understood that it was a matter of a new "branch" or "lodge" of their own Society. From the day when the independent and purely scientific character of the new organization was clearly apparent, and when it was seen that it was arousing more and more interest without making use of any philosophical etiquette, the solicitude that had surrounded my efforts seemed to me to diminish noticeably and even to turn into mistrust.

That was, without doubt, the attitude of a minority! Besides, I do not judge, I repeat, I do not defend any more! I simply state the facts!

But I am obliged to state that most of the obstacles laid across my path, and the most perfidious attacks to which I have been subjected, always had as their instigators certain influential members of the Belgian Theosophical Society. I could of course cite some names, but what purpose would that serve, other than to lay even more emphasis upon these attitudes of antipathy?

But, let us resume the history of the astrological movement created under our aegis! From being a quarterly, our Revue had become fortnightly, and it was already appearing in thirty-two pages instead of six. In order to assure the stability of its budget—and here is the origin of that "commercialization" for which I was reproached—I had created a sort of consultation bureau called "Eleusis" in memory of the ancient Mysteries of that name. A strange thing, and be it said in passing, these Mysteries, even that name **Eleusis**, have always exercised upon me an attraction that I cannot explain to myself! A simple coincidence? Some analogies of ideas? Or a confused recollection of a previous life? How to resolve that problem? That name **Eleusis** is magical in the highest degree. It is in fact formed of seven letters, that is two groups of three letters, **ele** and **sis**—where, in each case, the letter in the middle serves as a hinge between two identical letters—and a seventh, **u**, which in its turn makes a hinge between the two preceding groups. That name possesses a profoundly occult signification, and it encompasses an important group of symbols, in particular that of divinity in its most perfect and harmonious expression.

To return to the subject with which we are occupied, namely that of the legitimacy of remunerative consultations; it was in a way the question of astrological professionalism that presented itself: does an astrologer have the right to claim some fees for his work? For a long time, I myself had fought the entire idea of any sort of mercantilism, and I had studied a number of horoscopes gratuitously, but the great majority of the members of the Institute made me realize that by doing so I was neglecting a possible source of resources capable of definitively shoring up the more and more shaky budget of our organization. The persons who had hitherto contributed to it to keep it in balance seemed equally astonished that we would not dream of taking advantage of this important source of revenue; and I therefore had the impression that I was putting myself, in their opinion, in a false situation. Besides, I had already on numerous occasions, discussed the "commercialization" of astrology—to use the term employed by its adversaries—and I did not see how it could be judged more unfavorably, or in a manner more reprehensible, than for example that of medicine, or even more so, that of the priesthood. In a talk given in November 1927, an opportunity had even been given to me to formulate a suggestion that was daring for that time—that of forming a group of conscientious and competent astrologers, to whom one could guarantee some possibilities of a sufficient recompense. "One day it will come—and soon, I am sure," I said in closing, "when consulting an astrologer will be as much in vogue as consulting a physician.!"

In this business, it is one more time, it seems to me, as in a lot of other circumstances, that it is the point of view of the general public that proves to be improper. The general public, I have already said, tends to make idols of people that it raises upon a shield; it idealizes them, it lends them perfect sentiments, absolute virtues, in the shade of which it shelters its naïve faith. It doesn't wonder for an instant, because it lives in a complete utopia, that the matter exercises again its rights to the highest echelons of public life. For it, a savant is a kind of saint who owes it to himself to disdain all mercantile or utilitarian preoccupation. Consequently, in its eyes there are only two kinds of people: tradesmen and idealists. And in its mind an idealist is not able, without dishonoring himself, to be occupied with questions of money. We would try in vain to make it understand that there is a world between working to become richer and working to balance the budget of a philosophical or scientific entity. More conscious fundamentally of its rights than of its duties, it doesn't realize that it is committing an injustice when it requires a consultation to be free of payment when the community—which means itself—doesn't ensure the practitioner's livelihood in such a case. And, renewing the story of the straw and the beam,[20] since it would never be agreeable to working for free, it passes judgment quite candidly and submits it to the sanction of opinion.

The opportunity and the "admissibility" of professionalism were indeed examined and sanctioned by an affirmative vote during the course of a general assembly of the Institute that was held on the 20th of May 1928. The future indeed proved to us that we had viewed it correctly. In fact, the French astrological movement—a movement that, by a curious "coincidence," was created at the same time as ours in 1926—was never able to free itself from a kind of lethargy resulting from insufficient revenue. It professed a disinterest worthy of praise, but it completely misunderstood realities. How, in fact, to oblige someone to devote his time **gratuitously**, and in a regular manner, to a sort of scientific messiah-ism, when the struggle for life had become so hard and had monopolized his energies so much! Faced with such a situation, the most willing wound up by deadening themselves! Astrology loses there, when one tries to favor it. This policy proves itself to be one of a high ideal resulting in a perfect nonsense! It is only possible with the assistance of some real sponsors! But those, alas! have become rarer and rarer in our epoch of mercantilism and of the eclipse of spirit. And this mercantilism, this commercialism, have they not ended by taking hold of all the sciences in general, as well as almost all religions? Keep this in mind! There exists only one solution, which at the same time safeguards prestige and the scientific work life, it is a State subsidy. But when this subsidy, for one reason or another, cannot be anticipated, there remains only two alternatives: either to make an appeal to faith, which will only be worth what that faith itself is worth, or to try to ensure the convenient exploitation of the idea itself. In the first case, scientific prestige remains intact, but its realization is sprinkled with crossings and ruts. In the second case, the success most often assumes a

---

[20] Translator's Note. A saying of Jesus, recorded in Matthew 7:3.

commercial appearance, and it is only somewhat later—when the public acknowledges the excessiveness of its judgment—that a scientific rehabilitation occurs.

This is perhaps the moment to take into account that we had, although very doubtful of the results of our initiative, solicited a subsidy from the **University Foundation**. That was, without any doubt, a premature step; the subsidy was naturally refused to us.

Thus, the proof was once more furnished to us that to attain our goal, we could only count upon ourselves!

Then, having gone around in a veritable vicious circle, we found ourselves confronted again with the only possible alternative: to draw forth from astrology itself the indispensable resources to ensure its diffusion and to contribute to the realization of our goals.

But this perspective did not go without creating some backwash within our organization. Moreover, despite the stunning success encountered at the beginning, but not lasting very long; one felt that there was being born among certain ones of us that sort of passive indifference that precedes a final discouragement, but which is so distinctly prejudicial to the pursuit of a work undertaken in common.

Conflicts Between Astrology
and Occultism

Meanwhile, the study of astrology had put me in close contact
with the Rosicrucian Association,[21] another occult group, founded
at Oceanside, California, by Max Heindel, author of the *Message
of the Stars*. That association had centers in almost all countries; it
did not exist in Belgium, but the Paris Center invited me one day to
give a lecture there. Thus I made a more intimate acquaintance
with the program of that Community, which comprised, besides
the free teaching of astrology and occultism, the no less disinter-
ested curing of the sick. The methods employed for the latter end
were of a purely occult order; since each night the members of the
Rosicrucian Order would gather together to pray in their Temple at
Oceanside—some advanced students, some "invisible
aides"—knowing how to effect the conscious doubling of their
personality, displacing themselves near some patients who had
formally accepted this kind of intervention, and they worked actively to reestablish among them the normal play of vital exchanges.

One fact will show, more eloquently than any confused explanations, the efficacy of this curative method of a purely psychic order, in which at first the spirit refuses to believe.

Towards the end of the winter of 1926-1927, my little girl—she

---

[21] Now known as The Rosicrucian Fellowship.

was only one year old—contracted a cold that rapidly degenerated into bronchial pneumonia with the danger of otitis. One afternoon, she appeared to me to be so prostrated that I became uneasy; several members of the household were visited equally with the same sinister presentiment. Everything, however, had been tried. Was it necessary then to resign oneself to the inevitable? In her cradle the child seemed to be at death's door; her nostrils were pinched and blue; her color became ashen. Abruptly, in the middle of the night, an inspiration crossed my mind. I was skeptical, I admit, with regard to the possible success of the psychic intervention of "invisible aides." But in such a circumstance would one not let himself resort to such resolutions that were desperate, even illogical or ridiculous? Taking down the telephone, I feverishly dictated the text of a cablegram addressed to the Rosicrucian Association of Oceanside, in which I implored their aid.

Then, having tried everything that was in my power, I resumed, in a state of resignation, my watch beside the cradle.

The next day, no improvement had occurred; quite the opposite! Towards one p.m., however, when my wife had gone to get some refreshment, and I was remaining alone in the room sadly watching the face of my sick little child, she suddenly gave a sigh, opened her eyes, recognized me and smiled—a thing she had not done for several days!—the rose returned suddenly to her cheeks, she turned over and went back to sleep as if she were better!

But at the same time—and I experienced a true commotion!—it seemed to me that a vibration impossible to describe was shaking the atmosphere of the room; the rhythm of my own life found itself turned upside down, and I even believed for a moment that my heart was going to burst! Then, that sensation, entirely physical, gave way to a real transport of joy when I took account of the metamorphosis which had been effected in my daughter's condition – a change that was unexpected and not even hoped for!

But that succession of impressions of all sorts had been so rapid, so poignant, that it had not permitted me any reflection or any pangs of conscience! And it is only after some moments, during which I had asked myself what the reason could be for this unhoped-for improvement, that, in the manner of a flash of lightning, of an illumination, that I recalled my telegraphic appeal of the night before, and I thought "Oceanside."

That intervention was also confirmed some time later by a letter from the Headquarters of the Rosicrucian Association acknowledging the receipt of my cablegram and telling me that the "invisible aides" had done their best to come to my aid.

From that moment I conceived—is it necessary to say?—a sincere gratitude for the Oceanside Center, and our exchanges of views became more frequent and more intimate. They helped me powerfully in certain moral difficulties, and I never found my new friends in default when I asked them for a clarification or for advice. God knows, however, if I had recourse often to their good will; some others, at their place, would no doubt be worn out. But, on the contrary, Oceanside encouraged me ceaselessly to realize to the utmost the spiritual promises inherent in the grand trine of ASC-Neptune-conjunction-Sun-Mercury in my natal horoscope. I could certainly not have asked for better, but the task was not easy; for it is a fact—and the student of it is duly warned—that after he has made the first step on the occult path, he finds himself submitted to a material pressure very much stronger than any in the past. It is as if a powerful stream, hitherto held back by some dikes or by some sluices, should suddenly pour out with all the force of which it is capable. Also, the life of an occultist is, from the interior point of view, a field of continual battle!

This explains how, in my communications with Oceanside, a more and more profound sympathy had had its birth without, however, our ever having seen it. They obviously knew my name and some details of my current life; but I did not know, by contrast, even the sex or the title of the persons with whom I was maintaining a regular correspondence; for they signed their letters with their initials only. In fact the Order confined its members to the strictest anonymity in their propaganda work and their labor of healing; it wanted to present itself to the eyes of all as a sort of abstract symbol, although an active one, and not just a simple association of personalities. But such a sincerity, such a faith, such an unselfishness emanated from these epistolary communications that I had no fear of being obliged someday to regret the confidence of which I was thus giving proof.

As for the rest, I had the opportunity to enter into contact with some animators of the French Rosicrucian movement and a delegate of the Oceanside Center who was on a mission in Europe. Seldom did conversation reveal itself to be more fraternal and solicitude more unselfish! My gratitude and my esteem were again reinforced by it.

Because, no doubt, of the position that I had acquired in the Belgian astrological movement, I was sounded out soon after with regard to the creation of a Rosicrucian Center at Brussels. At first I had to decline that proposition, not wanting—besides not being able from an occult or moral point of view—to juxtapose such an initiative with my philosophic obligations to the Theosophical Society. I explained my situation to the General Headquarters at Oceanside, which not only understood my scruples very well, but approved of them totally.

But the Theosophical Society soon had to pass through a more grave moral crisis! Two of its principal directors, Mrs. Annie Besant and C.W. Leadbeater, had in effect solemnly proclaimed during the course of several years that, thanks to their faculties of clairvoyance, they had discovered the new Messiah in the person of a young Hindu, J. Krishnamurti [1895-1986]. An entire literature on this proclamation had seen the light of day; and a new Order, the "Order of the Star of the East," had been created with a view to preparing for the coming of the Instructor of the World.

The event seemed incredible; but the credibility that the "sponsors" of Krishnamurti inspired was such that the most skeptical took up a position with regard to this that it was proper to call a "favorable anticipation."

It was necessary for Krishnamurti himself—who, be it said in passing, revealed himself to be a spiritual person of the first order, perhaps one more evolved even than his official patrons—got his back up against the role that they had intended to make him play, in order to denounce that audacious maneuver, which could only be explained by an unhealthy ambition or by political motives.[22]

At a blow, my confidence found itself shaken—as was that of many other members too—and I no longer felt myself in harmony with the atmosphere of the Theosophical Society. I don't want to say that it no longer interested me—far from that! Men pass on, and works remain!—but I found, however, that it was abusive that they were demanding of the members of the Society, at the moment when they were admitted, a declaration of blind confidence in those in charge who were capable of lending themselves to such a game. Besides, my health at that moment left much to be desired; and, if the vegetarianism—which I had had to adopt in view of my occult enthusiasm—had accelerated the disintoxication following my bout with the flu, the cerebral and nervous overwork contributing to the said enthusiasm, combined with too strenuous physical labor, inclined me to suspend for the moment every practical formation. But, contrary to what one might suppose, perfect health was necessary to practice occultism effectively. Therefore, in 1929 I dissolved the ties binding me to the Theosophical Society.

From that moment on, I turned more and more toward the Rosicrucian Movement of Oceanside. Two years or more later, on the threshold of the winter of 1931, I founded the Rosicrucian Center of Brussels, and I began to give an oral course in astrology there. It was the beginning of an evolution that was going to draw me away from a pure and practical scientism towards some less rigid concepts, more in relationship with the occult teachings.

It had required all my gratitude to Oceanside to vanquish the scruples that had assailed me on that occasion. In fact I had to as-

---

[22] Translator's Note. Krishnamurti withdrew from the World Order of the Star and the Theosphical Society in 1929.

sault my temperament in order to accept dispensing a teaching that was above all a technique under a philosophical etiquette, as sympathetic as that one was for me. In effect, I ran the risk of creating a kind of opposition of attitudes between the concepts of the **Astrological Institute** and those of the new Center. In my eyes, the two attitudes were distinct; but would the profane always understand it? Without taking into account that I was creating a sort of dispersion or scattering of my activities in the same line of work.

But I had the satisfaction nevertheless of contacting in this fashion a public quite a bit different from that which I had known before, namely the public of spiritualists, animated by high ideals, and one that sought in astrology a means towards moral improvement. The utmost of fraternity, the most complete lack of partiality, presided at these meetings. It was obligatory to conform to the very strict directives of Oceanside in this matter, and it was also obligatory not to deviate from the principles of its philosophy or from its general mode of teaching. Among them, therefore, astrology was represented in the sense of a "revelation," a profession of faith, while at the Institute it was taught under the sign of free scientific discussion.

Another scruple tormented me again: it was that in the capacity of President of the said Rosicrucian Center I found myself personally subject to criticism, since in the meantime I had become a professional astrologer. I had been open with the General Headquarters at Oceanside, which, without totally approving,—since this had been absolutely contrary to their rule of conduct—had appreciated the logic of certain of my arguments and was showing itself extremely understanding of matters concerning the problem of material necessities. Our exchange of correspondence on that subject had been something of an epic! In short, it was not the professionalism in itself that could be criticized, but, from the special point of view—religious, in a way—which was that of the Rosicrucian Association, like that of the Theosophical Society too—every material demand formulated for work furnished creates a lien that hinders the expansion of the conscience, even if the said work has been done with the most generous spirit and with the purest intentions. According to the philosophical point of view in question, every action must be accomplished in a spirit of total altruism, and not in an anxiety of personal interest or competition. One can see that this point of view derives from the most pure Christianity; and, even if a lapse could justify itself by exceptional reasons, the example thus given ran the risk of being misinterpreted and of leading other persons into temptation. This is why the principle of non-reward must, in this philosophical concept, remain inviolable.

Is it plain that a supplementary conflict came to me as a result of this contradictory situation? On my advice, however—and that is one of the arguments that I had made to Oceanside—that concept, in order to be inviolable, would also have forbidden the sale of books at a fixed price; I said that these works would have had to be distributed free of charge, but with the distributor free to accept in return gifts or compensation freely agreed to. If the publisher, on the one hand, could pretend to recoup at least the cost of his purchases of paper, his printing and sales expenses, the astrologer, on the other hand, had a right to recover in the same fashion a guaranty of his general expenses, his documentation expenses, and even those of his labor. Once more there is a distinction drawn here between the honest practitioner, soliciting only a compensation for his consultation, and the maker of horoscopes exclusively preoccupied with making his own fortune, when this was done by exploiting the public credulity.

To still my conscience, I nevertheless tried to give some benevolent counsels, leaving to the beneficiary himself the task of fixing the price. Alas! experience showed itself to be deceptive, indeed disastrous: most of those involved restrained themselves from paying me; those with better intentions—ignorant no doubt of the fact that lengthy work was involved—graciously offered me a ten or twenty-franc bill.[23] At that rate, the Institute would quickly have been able to put an end to its activities!

---

[23] Translator's Note. Roughly equivalent to $5 or $10 today.

To return once more to the philosophical point of view with which we are concerned here, it is useless to remark that that point of view, while it was appreciated at its just moral value, would have enjoyed no credit at the Institute, where things were envisaged from a more positive angle. And likewise, more than a sticking point!—those who criticized us were of that happy lot whose civil position or well established personal fortune sheltered them from all imperious material preoccupations! It is easy to criticize, under those conditions! Besides, for us it was a matter before all else of convincing; and all the means permitting us to attain that end were, from that very fact, legitimate. As we were dealing especially with people of a strongly realistic spirit, our attitude was perfectly logical and without any possible equivocation. It could lend itself to regret or criticism only in the eyes of the pure spiritualists; but since those proceeded from a point of view that was very personal, and in some respects dogmatic, we would have no reason to rally ourselves to their concepts. Besides, we had no motivation to engage in polemics with them, since they were in the main already won over to the science that we were defending. Would to Heaven that they had always shown the same tolerance towards us that we thus gave proof of towards them!

The differences in teaching, of which I am now going to speak, did not, however,—as one can easily imagine—fail to lead to certain discussions at the heart of the new Rosicrucian Center. But they never raised up any truly serious echo; they remained internal—moral in a way—everyone showing himself to be understanding of the point of view of others. But the spirit that ought to preside in the Administration of a Center of that kind was necessarily suffering; at one moment I was on the point of stopping my classes—in which, I repeat, I was obligatorily contradicting certain details of my teaching at the Institute—and I even decided a little later, to resign at the proper time, at least as President. That resignation, which took place in 1935, did not spare the Brussels Center from counter blows of another sort—the new President, Mr. Bottelbergs, having wished to provoke a schism! But the ordeals only disturbed the weak! Our Center, which was strong, happily resisted and little by little developed an excellent internal atmosphere under the management of its present President, Mr. Toussaint.

May I take this opportunity, before abandoning the subject, to make a brief allusion to a conference that I held at the said Center, and which shows to what degree I had to be careful in the expression of its thought. I had discussed in this review, life in the U.S.S.R., and I had set forth with an unfeigned sympathy certain social measures that had been instituted there; I had done this, it must be said, with a purely philosophical and humanitarian end in mind, and not with any political end. Some members of the audience showed themselves to be very interested; but others were indignant—they saw in that a failure in the disciplines of the Association, they denounced it to the General Headquarters and thus contributed to increasing my reputation of being an *enfant terrible*! I even had to furnish some explanations to Oceanside, and to reestablish the facts as to the exact line of my intentions. Presently, I evidently showed myself more defiant; but that defiance was not in my nature, and—it will be seen presently—somewhat later I ran up yet again against some analogous experiences.

Let us admit that I had shown myself a little free in my choice of subject, when some themes that were quite as attractive were not lacking in the Rosicrucian literature! But the demonstrative and current point of view has always seduced me in defense of an idea; and I always show myself as a militant before all else. This is doubtless the effect of the Mercury-Uranus square in my chart, as well as the Moon-Mars conjunction in Sagittarius. But when I muse on that, I can only deplore with a touch of bitterness that fate that obliges me to think regularly "on the margin" of the common herd, always slow to render an account of myself, and prone to judge things on the opposite side of the general opinion. I will have an opportunity to cite other examples of this in the course of these "Confidences."

I said above, apropos of the scruples that inspired me in my post as President of the Brussels Rosicrucian Center, that I had in the meantime become a professional astrologer. In fact, astrology had finally monopolized me to such a degree that from 1926 on I was at the same time managing the direction of the Institute, the *Eleusis* office, my courses, my conferences, the editing of the Revue—its publication and that of my own works—at the same time as the administration of a big Anglo-international society, which was not just a sinecure. I inevitably found it necessary from time to time to neglect something, nor was it only the details, while the clearest and most certain result was to overwork myself, sometimes to the point of total exhaustion. I acknowledged that that was an absurd attitude, and more absurd besides since I always felt the effects of my influenza, which, although already remote, ought to have incited me to take certain cautions. But I have already remarked that these excesses of work derived from the intellectual passion that astrology inspired in me.

And then it was necessary to work doubly hard to do the work and fulfill the responsibilities that lay more and more heavily on my shoulders alone. General Buisset died in 1927; Mr. Chapellier, always partial to new studies, seemed, as a perfect native of the sign Libra, to have a passion for other horizons; more particularly, he had just founded the periodical **Uranus** and a new movement **"The Collaboration"**; Mr. De Landtsheer, more and more hermetic, had returned to his "ivory tower" and would hardly consent any more to leave it. As for Mr. Nicolay, who had replaced General Buisset on the Council, he did not hide his aversion to the new orientation taken by the activities of the Institute.

In short, from the fact of having set in motion a task that ended by becoming overwhelming, I found myself quite constrained to fulfill it, under the pain of seeing the results of so much effort definitely compromised. But besides I felt more acutely that a new solution was indispensable to a short delay.

Certain difficulties of administration having occurred in the Society that I was directing, I used that for a pretext to break in 1930, after seven years of collaboration, the contract that tied me to it. However, I sacrificed there a magnificent situation, and with a little wisdom on my part, I would certainly have been able to continue to carry on my professional occupations side by side with my astrological amateurism. But I have said previously that I hold some rather absolute views in all things, and I suffered morally from not being able to devote myself any longer to the science that had become for me an imperious mistress.

I was therefore very happy to free myself thus from all commercial attachment, and, after a well-deserved vacation, I believed it opportune to open an office in the center of Brussels. Understandably, I went through a period of groping, difficulties, and doubts; and I only broke progressively from my profession. So that after some months, I felt that, from a practical point of view, the field of astrology presented itself favorably. From then on I devoted my efforts exclusively to the Institute and to its diverse activities. Financially speaking, I lost a lot there; but the task pleased me, and that compensated for that.

It was no longer a question, starting from that moment, of sporadic work, improvisations, and chance solutions. My own destiny was now tied to that of the organization created four years earlier. It was going to be necessary to concentrate its efforts, take some risks, and accentuate the propaganda. It was a new step that was opening!

Fifteen Years of Professionalism

This stage of professionalism is the most fruitful of my life, but also the most agitated. I am constantly on the battle-line. Propaganda, teaching, the Revue, balancing the budget, the maintenance of numerous relationships, both internal and external, producing continuous problems, in the sense that they constituted "dead" activities that have to be supported by those activities that are properly called professional. In other words, the support of the Belgian astrological movement appears to be very burdensome, in money as well as in effort; and my own personal projects are already put in second place.

I soon realized that I had made a mistake in settling myself in the center of town. Almost every day there is a steady stream of curiosity seekers whom it is necessary to give information to; it is only when evening comes that I can begin to work effectively. If I looked sullen from the effort, I often had bitter reflections on the desire that had driven me to free myself from all supervision in order to devote myself entirely to the furtherance of my ideas; for here I am now, independent, but more enslaved than ever! I have simply changed masters: the public, capricious and demanding, determines my leisure time and my tasks!

The first of my cares has been to find out how to establish, in the form of a loan, a basis of cash-flow for the Institute. Already, for a couple of years, the Viscount de Herbais de Thun had joined his efforts with mine, and he had become a member of the Administrative Council; he declares that he is agreeable to advance—and if necessary, to lose!—a sum of five thousand francs.[24] I agreed to do the same. Two other of our most devoted members, Miss Baert of Antwerp, and Mrs. G., who were in a position to do so, offered to complete the necessary capital. Thus, we assembled a fund of twenty thousand francs.[25] It was not very much, but with good management, and especially with a little luck, that amount could suffice.

Alas! After several months of feverish activity, and in spite of an undeniable success and with general expenses reduced as much as possible, the accounts revealed a loss of more than 19,000 francs![26] You might as well say that the capital was entirely lost! My associates had moreover long since resigned themselves to the loss of their investment; they were waiting from one day to another for the liquidation of our glorious enterprise!

Discouraged by this situation, on one day that seemed more somber than the others, I declare that I am abandoning this tiring combat!

At that moment, I am dreaming of that high functionary who had put me so much on guard some years too soon and who would rebuke me with "Nothing can be done in Belgium! You are going to wear yourself out in a struggle that will lead to nothing!" How right he was!

For two whole days, I pass alternately through rage and despair. It is a tremendous disappointment for me! Is it necessary, then, for me, after having found a chosen living in the passionate dynamism that possessed me, to take up a commonplace existence again, to renew my interest in some strictly administrative or commercial

---

[24] Translator's Note. In the late 1920s, 5,000 Belgian Francs was the equivalent of U.S. $700, which, allowing for inflation, would have the purchasing power of about $14,000 in today's money.

[25] Translator's Note. About U.S. $2,800, with an equivalent purchasing power of U.S. $56,000 in today's money.

[26] Translator's Note. About U.S. $2,660, the equivalent of U.S. $53,200 in today's money.

activities?

On the third day,—is the Sun warmer, more brilliant, the air more alive?—I suddenly regain my confidence, I feel that I have become optimistic! I recall that often already the meager budget of the Institute has been in difficulty, and that on each occasion some happy circumstance has intervened to put it back afloat. And I decide, come what may, to pursue the adventure; for that is what it really is!

To do so, it is necessary to reduce expenditures even more; I impart to my associates my intention to close my office in downtown Brussels and to transfer it to my home, which would already effect an important economy. They let me do as I wish, resigned to the worst, not having anything more to lose.

The transfer is accomplished; some personal economies are realized; the work continues in a more tranquil environment; it becomes more effective and consequently more remunerative. Little by little, the loss is reduced, and the day arrives when the Institute, having repaid the loan that had been made to it, can live on its own course and on its own capital.

From then on, from a financial point of view, the history of our Association would unroll without any notable incident down to the outbreak of the recent Great War. There would indeed be some serious declines in the curve of receipts; but always, these alarms would be of short duration and followed by abrupt resumptions. Thus, it will be seen that the Institute develops following an ascending curve down to the day when, due to one of those excessive scruples which are common to me, I would contemplate dividing it into two distinct organizations.

In fact, the reproach that was made to me about commercializing astrology had touched me profoundly because of its illogic and even its injustice. And as, since 1930, I had pushed that "commercialization"—I would say: that "professionalism"!—at the most, I intend to remain logical within myself and to limit the scope of that criticism as much as possible.

Since 1930, I had in fact launched astrology on a new field of battle: the domains of the Stock Market. And certainly that is the abomination of desolation! I, who passed willingly for an idealist, or even an altruist, I was there fallen into the last echelon of sordidness! And the slanders followed in course! It is entirely fair, if I am not put in the rank of "fakirs," "professors," and other merchants of horoscopes in series!

I shall explain myself presently, in more detail, about the end I pursued by introducing astro-dynamics into the financial domain. It is not as interesting as some have wanted to believe; and the proof of that is that I have not gotten rich. Still, it is a cause of astonishment for a number of people, and apropos of which it will be suitable for me to furnish some clarifications.

Everyone doesn't overwhelm me, fortunately! With the entry of Mr. de Herbais de Thun into the Administrative council of the Institute, it finally has a weighty and extraordinarily devoted and active element. Then, Messers Chapellier and Nicolay having ceased their collaboration—the one for lack of time, the other for divergence of views—a new and particularly dynamic administrator, Mr. Guy Onkelinx joined us. Without respite, he encourages our efforts, he makes us benefit from his numerous relations, incites us to show the public, by some constantly renewed experiences, the whole part that it can draw from astrological science. Under his impulse, some conferences followed by demonstrations are given every week, and followed by some selected public lectures, the *Revue* itself—which meanwhile has taken a new title *Demain*—gets better steadily, it gains in its presentation and quality. Its predictions and its monthly guide are followed by some readers, more and more numerous, who are passionately interested in marking the points. In fact, we fairly regularly record some good "successes"; and it must also be said that our articles are particularly studied and polished.

The controversy is mixed, in other respects! Certain scientists, carried away by their rank prejudice, take offense at our success. They try to discredit us in the eyes of the public; but we defend ourselves with asperity, and our fencing is not inferior to that of our detractors. A particularly close duel takes place thus in the arena of the satirical newspaper *Pourquoi Pas?* We are very flattered on this occasion to learn that the Review *Demain* is passing the point of having around 50,000 readers!

In short, the movement in favor of astrology, launched timidly in 1926, has now grown stout and is developing rapidly. We are beginning to have to balance a very sizable budget, and my responsibilities are becoming heavier and heavier, the Review now absorbs considerable sums on its own. The revenues fortunately, are rising in proportion, and that permits us to enlarge in a technical sense the limits of our publication, by introducing in it some articles that remain outside of the view of the average reader, but which on the other hand interest the student and interested parties. The latter finally then find their benefit in the exploitation of that somewhat "hybrid" formula.

But, to return to the legal history—as it were—of the Institute, I finally realized that, for a non-profit Association, the profitable activities begin to be particularly dominant. Evidently,—but at that moment it did not appear so!—that scruple is excessive and almost ridiculous! It is taking things too literally! All the A.S.B.L. have a commercial activity, and even those that have a religious goal do not experience returns of similar conscience. One has seen since then some disguises and some otherwise flagrant abuses: in a world in which the decline of morality overturns all logic and annihilates all propriety, that there was nothing more in honor at the moment to circumvent the Vandervelde law[27] than the famous "private circles" created under the form of non-profit associations, when it was a question, plainly enough, of common sales of alcohol, which could not be more mercantile!

That is what it is to be born under the Saturnian influence! One cultivates some rigid principles, the moral is rather susceptible, and some scruples are derived from it that would truly be more

---

[27] Translator's Note. Evidently a law passed by the Belgian Socialist Minister Émile Vandervelde (1866-1938) levying a tax on alchoholic beverages.

proper in some otherwise important circumstances! Besides, the influence of Aquarius pushes me pitilessly to desire perfection, and I [cannot] stop [trying] that everything that I have undertaken is presented in the best way. Also, the ordinary people and those concerned about their ease consider me with fright!

On my suggestion, we decided then in 1935 to re-establish the Institute in its primitive "purity," by bringing to this end all the actually commercial activities to a cooperative Society. since five years the group of active collaborators of the Institute had grown by some units; cooperation had always been a principle of our work—not [that] of a hierarchy in the proper sense of the word—not of a convict-gang!—[but simply] of the sort that we want to continue to work in the same spirit.

It should be said in passing that cooperation is an excellent method of administration, on the condition that each one approaches his task in the same spirit; otherwise, one day there are some profiteers and some who are injured! But once more, my theme explains why that form of administration has always seduced me, in spite of the inevitable disappointments: the sign of Aquarius gives a sense of collaboration, even in an advanced spirit, and that of Pisces confers much more indulgence than severity. Besides, a Vensusian is very naturally hostile to a rigorous and strictly hierarchical discipline. Of course, that doesn't go as far as a total naivety because of my Saturn!

The cooperative Society that had just been founded at the end of 1935 under the name **Les Éditions de la Revue Demain** grouped together then all of the activities that related to the Review itself, to its publications, to astrological consultations, and to financial bulletins; in short, everything that, without including whatever it is that is really mercantile—the concern for the science and for our good renown always comes first—is susceptible of returns of a commercial order.

The Institute itself, will no longer constitute a symbol of rallying only for astrologers, a center of documentation and teaching.

Moreover, the statutes of the new Society foresee a sort of yearly subsidy in its favor. Therefore, no reproach of "commercialization" can any more be addressed to it; on the other hand, we will note later that, by this separation that removes from it some important financial resources, we have placed it in the cataleptic attitude of the "Astrological Society of France." And, to cap it all, we will even be blamed one day for this apparent inactivity! In fact, the public manifestations of the institute will stop almost completely, but they will continue to express themselves as oral and written teaching, as well as in the accumulation of a considerable documentation.

A nursery of remarkable students is formed thus; our courses comprise three years of studies, at the end of which every pupil, having satisfied the final examination—and that examination is not a simple formality, the candidates know that!—obtains a diploma in good and due course.

There then are some new talents, some new persons of good will taking their place in the cohort that wages the good fight for astrology! Some, because of the fact of their knowing that they will be free of all tutelage thereafter, will want to skip some stages, animated as they are by that enthusiasm that is a little fanatic that characterizes prophets as part of their vocation; and, faced with their audacities, we will have our eye astonished like the mother hen who sat on a duck egg! But time has an effect, and with the sense of moderation coming to them little by little, they finally in their turn do work that is truly useful; it is essential, for enthusiasm is a virtue that is too rare today for even its excesses to be blamed. Besides, only those who have the sacred fire within them can become masters and can plow the furrow from which the future harvests will sprout!

During that time, the cooperative Society prospers, and the number of its collaborators always grows. But it is soon going to have to transform its legal form again.

The Internal Revenue Service, in effect, does not conceive cooperation in the [same] spirit that everyone does; it interprets things and agreements according to the interests of the Treasury! Considering our society in its form and not in its spirit, it therefore contests its cooperative character under the pretext that our statutes do not foresee any refunds at the end of the year in favor of our members. Now, the eventual profits of the exercise were shared between the cooperators in proportion to the material contributions and work done by each of them! In short, we were taxed in such a way, and grief-stricken by such a "bleeding," that it was only left for us to assure ourselves of some normal tax rates: the one that designated us as a Corporation.

That was in my eyes, from the idealistic point of view, the most abominable solution, but what else was there to do? At the end of 1937, the **Éditions de la Revue Demain** then became a corporation with a capital of fifty-three thousand francs!

There ended the succession of periodical transformations of our institution. Some accessory incidents naturally occurred in other domains. Then, there was the war, that curiously shook us up and actually constituted for us what could be for a ship on the high seas in an equinoctial tempest!

It was thus that our co-worker of the moment, Antarès, a fine fellow and a capable astrologer, but very unstable in mood and of a sometimes excessive touchiness, left us suddenly for no very good reason, and even tried to establish an organization entirely resembling ours. We didn't take offense at it, Belgium being big enough to nourish two or even more astrological Studios; in fact, and since our advertising was doing its work, the possible "clientele," was automatically increasing. Why would we have had any need in those conditions to fear a "rivalry"?

A counter-attack would have been easy, however, if we had wanted to make one; it would have sufficed to stop the sale of his *Manuel d'Astrologie*. Persuaded to act thus in the general interest, while showing to Antarès that he kept us strictly in the wrong, we continued to reissue that work until all copies had been sold. Was that not the best attitude to take?

Besides, it is necessary to give justice to Antarès, since he ended by admitting that a good understanding among astrologers was well worth the sacrifice of pride on his part. And, after some mutual explanations, peace was made again.

Aside from that, our small team continued to make progress as a very homogeneous whole.

More fabulous is the history of that review of astrology and occultism called **Revelations,** founded by some journalists of my relations, Mr. Watelet, A. Michel, and Mr. Lecomte, and to which I was "summoned" in a friendly way to take part. Without having been able to take into account what was going on, I even found myself one day promoted without any notice to a sort of dignity—that of Editor in Chief—a dignity that was only maintained, at my request, until the next issue appeared!

That review, which did not lack some quality, unfortunately had only an ephemeral existence; in fact, it suffered from being "botchy" and excessively casual. Towards the end, the *Dictionnaire infernal* of Collin de Plancy [1794-1881], and even certain works protected by copyright, were cut up into slices! The Revue *Revelations* died from the lack of care that often afflicts infants whose birth has not been ardently desired; but such as it was, it had nevertheless acquired the sympathy of the public.

Perhaps it is interesting to note here that the Revue **Revelations,** that appeared after the liberation under the aegis of Miss Demain (a curious coincidence...) had no relationship close or distant with the one of which I am going to speak, and even less with the Revue *Demain.* I am perhaps getting ahead of myself, but that is a fixed point in history! And having thus trimmed down the history of the **Institut belge d'astrologie scientifique** and that of the **Société des Éditions de la Revue Demain,** let us return to some earlier years to take up the question of who brought about the "diverse movements"—that of the application of astrology to investments in equities.

Astrology at the Bank of Proof of the Stock Exchange

It was by having been struck by some celestial concordances that existed between the crash and the death of the Belgian financier Loewenstein [1877-1928] and the natal chart of the latter that the idea of a possible correlation between matters of finance and astral influences anchored themselves in my mind. Without doubt, I was not the only one to take note of this![28] But it was a question of building these correlations into a system and of "codifying" in some manner the rules that were discovered.

The Loewenstein crash, of sinister memory, occurred on September 4, 1928, under a Mars-Jupiter conjunction, which is often the indication of a serious disturbance of the stock market. One of the stocks of the Loewenstein group, the "Brazilian Traction," showed itself to be particularly sensitive to the conjunction and to the parallel of these two planets; nine times out of ten, then it plainly revealed an unexpected downward deviation.

But for this it was necessary to consider the problem through the small end of the glass, and the synthesis took some time to appear to me clearly. Besides, I only studied the problem at intervals

---

[28] Translator's Note. See for example the information on Alfred Loewenstein in Maurice Privat, *Finanz-giganten* [Giants of Finance] (Leipzig: E.A. Seemann, 1929). His birthdata is given in English in Lois Rodden's *Astro-Data III* (Tempe, Ariz.: A.F.A., Inc, 1986), pp. 238-239. He was bom at Brussels 11 Mar 1877 at 2 P.M. and fell (or was pushed) from his private plane into the sea and drowned in July 1928.

from 1928 to 1930, and, at that time, I had still only deduced a certain number of the laws that seemed to me to constitute already the "end of the end." They would, however, soon reveal themselves to be notoriously imperfect, and indeed insufficient.

I believed then prematurely that I had found the key to infallible speculations. But when, in 1930, instigated almost in spite of myself,—on the advice of my broker friend and based on some fallacious successes—to put my system into practice, I ventured to experiment in the market for the first time, I experienced one of those losses that disabuses you at once of every excessive delusion. For me, who had hoped, thanks to some fortunate speculations, to render the Institute safe from all risk, this was a harsh revelation! Struck in my scientific pride, I digested my discomfiture in silence; and I had thus the spare time to improve totally, by daily experiments, my system of predicting the movements of the market.

It was at the beginning of 1931 that for the first time I published the *Bulletins financiers* [Financial Bulletins], whose publication has not been interrupted since that time.

What was my reason for publishing these predictions, which were certainly going to arouse great interest among some persons, and the cruelest skepticism among others? Without taking into account the reproaches of those who, considering astrology as a religion, would find that this new application of it constituted a sacrilege!

Until that time, I had limited myself to applying astro-dynamics to the study of character, to the chances for success, to choosing a profession, to physiological questions, to the possibilities of understanding in conjugal matters or in matters of association. But in those subjects, there was in my eyes a sufficiently subjective means of convincing proof. Yet in fact, is there anything more debatable than the analysis of character? The very words are the source of equivocation, of imprecision, and of false interpretation; and then, anyone can always maintain that the astrologer has deformed things! On the contrary, with the Stock Market, I possessed a means of **objective** persuasion, resting upon facts that were obvious and almost mathematical—namely on figures.

If in fact one announces the low for this period of time, and that low appears, that is an indisputable proof of the validity of the system—at least, if the "coincidence" repeats itself with a sufficient regularity. And so, if I succeeded in forecasting with a satisfying approximation the market movements and their timing almost exactly, the proof would have been made that the stars do influence the market quotations. After that, the rest would follow automatically.

In short, my passion for astrology joined together there with my desire for accountability and mathematics. It was Saturn, rigorously positive that demanded of the solution of an astrological problem that it be the most unassailable, the most palpable, but also the most difficult!

There was then there, in the forefront of my thought—and however legitimate that could be—no concern about personal interest; and those who thought that there was have taken into consideration only the appearance itself of the facts. Without doubt—I admit it at the outset—I was favoring certain audacious speculators, I was lowering astrology to a rather material role; but what was the harm in these things with regard to the goal pursued and the revived interest in favor of astrology? The spiritualist movement, today so decried by the occultists, was well conceived originally in some analogous intentions, despite the risks and dangers that could spring from them. Every scientific discovery thus exhibits a two-edged sword depending upon the usage to which it is put. Look at dynamite, aviation, atomic energy, and so on!

Is it not their utilization for the purpose of murder or war that gives all their value to these discoveries, and permits them to render more fruitful the years of peace that follow?

Meanwhile, people are quite often astonished that I myself am not yet retired in a chateau in the country, living comfortably on the dividends derived from my stock market profits!

There is a thing that the common herd is unaware of, and that too many astrologers themselves forget: it is that financial success is before all else a function of the natal configurations. Now, whoever would like to study my horoscope even a little will soon perceive that if my Venus is favorable in principle to speculative matters,—I say *in principle*, because Venus is scarcely acting by herself—her action is compromised or vitiated by the square that she forms with Neptune. This aspect can be translated by the words: hesitations, influential maneuvers, laissez-faire, pernicious counsels, the lack of agreed upon decisions, insufficient moderation or balance, etc. Furthermore, Uranus in the 2nd house, in opposition—very fortunately—to my Jupiter, the natural significator of wealth, ruler of my 5th house, and placed in the 8th, does not naturally improve that diagnostic!

In fact, during the short period during which I tried, in spite of everything, to belie my horoscope, it happened that I realized exceptional gains on certain days. But, at other times, instead of following my own convictions, I let myself gain from the very different advice of my broker or from an adverse atmosphere. Or indeed to be more precise, too impatient—look at Mercury square Uranus! —I would be irritated that a movement would not launch itself at the exact moment I had foreseen, and I would extricate myself in a fit of excessive apprehension, only to discover in the days following that by doing so I had committed a regrettable error.

It will be said that I was lacking faith in my system! That is certainly not the case, since the market advisories that I was giving out were revealed to be exact and largely profitable for those who had the turn of mind necessary to take advantage of it! But at that time, I had not understood the imperious necessity that exists of knowing how to isolate oneself in such a case from the market atmosphere; and, too confident in others' experience, I sometimes let myself be influenced, or I evaded [my own advice]; or even there occurred one of those particularly embroiled combinations of circumstances that are indeed inherent in the nature of Neptune, and my best conceived plans very narrowly failed. I had the experience, for example, of buying some options, of seeing them rise as I had foreseen, but not sufficiently to give me a profit after my costs were deducted.

—It can be seen then that the problem presents itself in a manner that is very much more complicated than is generally supposed! Agreed! But someone will raise an objection for me here—let us admit that you were not born for speculation in the market; but these financial subscriptions had to make some big returns for you?

—"I do not deny it," I will reply, but the receipts from the *Bulletins* pass into the budget of the Society, where they serve to cover the general expenses and the deficits of certain departments, namely the *Revue*. Therefore, I would not profit from them directly; and besides, without them we would never have been able to pursue the struggle for our ideas for as long as we did.

The Financial Bulletins knew some remarkable successes, and they provided me with a prodigious number of experiences, some of them extraordinarily instructive, and others simply amusing or picturesque, and still others definitely disagreeable. I intend to say some more about this further on in the chapter in which I set forth some of my most curious recollections.

All of the observational principles that relate to the application of astrology to the Stock Market are found together in my work *Fluctuations boursières et Influences cosmiques* [Stock Market Fluctuations and Cosmic Influences], a second edition of which, revised and augmented, emanated from the press during the last war. May I be permitted to say about this that if I had been as sordidly involved as certain people have pretended, I would certainly not have put the results of my lengthy researches and my costly experiences within the reach of everyone. On the contrary, I would have reserved that information for myself alone, and I would have exploited it on a grand scale. My method of action, on the contrary, has rather disconcerted—I noted it time and again—certain financiers, who seemed to be in agreement that I did not possess any normal reflexes. And, indeed, they were perhaps entirely correct!

Besides, why would I not have shown in this case an astrological "factory," following the example of so many French or Dutch "professors" or "fakirs"? I had an opportunity to do so without any risk! One day, in fact, I received a visit from a stranger who offered me the opportunity to take charge of an enterprise of that sort in Paris. Pretending to be interested in his proposition, I inquired about the possible financial reward if I accepted.

—"Two hundred percent of the advertising figure," he replied.

Now, some similar enterprises paid each year on average one or two million francs for advertisement in the big dailies. In other countries, at an elevated rate, this figure is increased to 10 or 15 million. it can be seen then that the offer was seductive! But I dismissed my visitor politely, while explaining to him that in my eyes my reputation was worth more than a fortune, no matter how great, gained under those conditions.

In all sincerity, I must admit that he did not show himself to be overly surprised by my negative response, for which he seemed to have been prepared. He only inquired whether, among my associates, I could recommend someone whom I would judge suitable to fill the rule that he had in mind.

And here I may be permitted, parenthetically, a reflection that seems to me to be entirely appropriate. When one considers the success won among the general public by these fabricators of horoscopes—it is known that they receive from three to four thousand requests each day, which already fetches them each morning something like ten thousand francs in postage stamps "to cover the cost of a reply"!—one notes that this success derives directly from a perfect knowledge of mass psychology. Which, as I said in a previous chapter, takes pleasure in putting on a pedestal those who seem to produce some work of science, religion, or philanthropy. Now, it is not out of philanthropy to offer, as these "fakirs," "professors," and other charlatans do, a "free" horoscope in return for the derisory sending of two or three francs in stamps? These good people are evidently ignorant of the fact that the material cost of the "horoscope" that they receive is already largely covered by this amount, as small as it is. And that it is thereafter, at the time of a second consultation, that these tradesmen make up for it! Then one sees the figure of these fees to rise suddenly up to several hundred francs. And note that all these figures that I have mentioned are pre-war figures! What will this be when they have been equated to present day rates?

Meanwhile, and to return to the astrological movement, properly said, a great progress—which it will be necessary for me to review in more detail at an opportune moment—had marked the period following 1930. First of all, the review *Demain* had enlarged its format and increased the number of pages—it had finished by appearing each month in 48 pages; the number of its subscribers and readers had also remarkably increased. Each month, it went forth to all the countries of the world, even the most remote, indeed to little islands lost in the expanse of the Pacific or in the China Sea, that it was necessary to locate on an atlas. I must say, besides, that we were doing everything within our power to make our publication interesting and to give it a serious character. We had at certain times added to it some exclusively technical *Supplements*, which appeared every three months; but there our initiative encountered too great an indifference, and we were obliged to stop that kind of publication after two years, which had resulted in a sensible loss.

Our [other] publications had also found a very favorable reception among the public. After O. De Landtsheer's work, *Comment dresser votre horoscope* [How to Cast your Horoscope], which rapidly sold out, I had published *Contribution à l'étude de l'astro-dynamique* [A Contribution to the Study of Astro-Dynamics], a book that was unfortunately printed in too small a number of copies, and because of this, it consequently rose to a prohibitive price in the bookstores. Then, *Fluctuations boursières et Influences cosmiques* [Stock Market Fluctuations and Cosmic Influences] appeared. The Viscount de Herbais de Thun had brought out on his side two remarkable works: *Synthèse de l'Oeuvre de Choisnard* [Synthesis of the Work of Choisnard] and *Synthèse de l'Interprétation astrologique* [Synthesis of Astrological Interpretation]. Next there came the *Manuel pratique d'Astrologie scientifique* [Practical Manual of Scientific Astrology] by our fellow worker Antarès, which book, presented in a classical and methodical manner, has realized a remarkable success, since it is now going into its fifth edition. Meanwhile, we had also published *Astrologie mondiale* [Mundane Astrology] by Léon Lasson, *Lumières sur l'Interprétation astro-chirologique* [Insights on Astro-chirological Interpretation] by Jean Léonard; and, a little before the recent war, we issued *Tables de Positions planétaires* [Tables of Planetary Positions] by the German mathematician K. Schoch, with a commentary translated from the German by R. Brihay, the third administrator of our Society. Of an entirely different genre, the Review *Demain* had also published a novel from my own pen, *A la Rencontre du Temps* [About an Encounter with Time], since republished under the title *Le Gardien du Seuil* [The Guardian of the Threshold], and, following my trip to America, to the Astrological Congress in New York in 1937—of which I will speak further—there had appeared *En Touriste aux Etats-Unis* [On Tour in the United States], a romanced account that received a truly flattering reception from both the press and the public, and which was also honored by the official approval of the Minister of Public Education. That work, which has seen its third edition, seems destined for a good career.

What else should I say to complete the list of our activity down to 1940? In 1939, the Review *Demain* established a prize of 5,000 francs designed to reward the best work or memoir that would provide a proof of astral influence in the scientific sense of the word; then, a proof that would be both objective and capable of repetition. The jury, of which Mr. A. Piccard, the well-known savant, kindly agreed to accept the presidency, also included two other professors of the University of Brussels, Mr. Cox (now, the Rector) and Mr. Staehl, and two astrologers, the Viscount de Herbais and myself. Ten memoirs were presented, and the Committee held several full sessions. It is unlikely that even one of the works presented would have been retained, the jury revealing themselves to be very skeptical and very demanding—that could be relied upon!—but in any case, the day after the entry of the German troops into Belgium, professor Piccard left for Switzerland, instructing one of his colleagues to return to us the memoirs that had been presented, so that the decision of the jury was postponed *sine die*.

In order to be complete, it remains for me to mention the presentation, in July 1932, at Brussels, at the 56th Congress of the **French Association for the Advancement of Science**, a memoir on the correlations that had been established between astral influences and the variations of prices in the Stock Markets. That memoir, which preceded the publication of my work, **Fluctuations boursières et Influences cosmiques** [Stock Market Fluctuations and Cosmic Influences] was only accepted thanks to the courtesy and broadmindedness of Mr. Max-Léo Gérard, who presided over the Economics Section of the said Congress, and to whom I am happy to be able to express here publicly all my thanks. Yet, my memoir had been baptized for that occasion with a title that was quite reassuring: ***Des Concordances qui existent entre les Crises économiques et certains Phénomènes du Monde physique*** [Some Concordances that Exist between Economic Crises and Certain Phenomena of the Physical World]. It was accepted, it must be said, with diverse sentiments; but nevertheless it contributed in a large measure to the penetration of my theories into banking and industrial circles.

This having been said, I do not believe that I have forgotten anything essential in this statement of our activities from 1930 to 1940. It would certainly have been possible to do better! But, given the feeble means at our disposal and the inertia of opinion with respect to new ideas, the reader will agree that the results obtained are encouraging and that they compensate us for efforts agreed upon and the vexations that we endured.

Now, I will view some particular aspects and some more anecdotes of my astrological activities. That will be the subject of the chapters that follow.

About the International Conventions under the Shadow of the Swastika

Incontestably, and thanks especially to the luster of the periodical *Demain* and to its good reception, the Belgian astrological movement had acquired a place of the first rank in the concert of world attention. Also, contacts that were more and more numerous and more and more methodical had been established with the astrologers of other countries. I shall cite at random those whose acquaintance I made during the "epic" period: **K. E. Krafft**, the remarkable Swiss researcher, whose tragic destiny was not foreseen at that moment; **Eudes Picard**, astonishing in his intuition; **Magi Aurélius**, Jupiterian and genial; **Mrs. Gine Brahé**, a remarkable adept at symbolic directions; **Col. Maillaud**, always helpful and welcoming, but a little bit of a dilettante; **Henri J. Gouchon**, always modest, but obstinately inclined towards his own investigations; **J. Reverchon**, at once a mathematician, a skeptic, and vehement; **Rigel**, a classic astrologer; **Dr. Korsch** of Düsseldorf, erudite and decisive; **P.J. Harwood**, pink-complexioned and chubby, remarkably intuitive; **E. Hentges**, a Luxembourg astrologer, methodical and precise. I pass over and no doubt forget others, may they excuse me, who would be too numerous to mention. But be assured that we were in correspondence with hundreds of researchers in all five parts of the world.

It was only later, on the occasions of the international conventions that I had the opportunity to make the acquaintance of other well-known astrologers, such as **A. Volguine, M. Privat, Janduz, W. J. Tucker, R. Gleadow, E. Thierens, E. Kühr**, and **Mrs. Yvonne Tritz**, to name only a few. These relationships, thanks to the valuable collaboration that they brought to our movement, had the effect of intensifying the dynamism and interest of the periodical *Demain*. Also, it is thanks to them that Viscount de Herbais de Thun was able to do so well with his project, the *Encyclopédie du Mouvement astrologique de langue française.*

One country, to my mind, especially distinguished itself by its dynamism; that country—and I am a little confused to feel obliged to render it homage at the moment when the scandal of the extermination camps has come out to tarnish its reputation in the civilized world—was Germany, where numerous periodicals, of diverse inspirations, worked for the good cause. One of them especially seemed to me to have placed itself at the forefront of the movement: the periodical *Zenit*, directed by Dr. Korsch. I don't know whether my opinion is the same as that of the German astrologers, but it seemed to me that that publication, very serious, very scientific, and mainly very technical—which excluded for example all those features of which the public is so fond: predictions, daily guides, etc.—was the most representative of those that appeared across the Rhine. In any case, it was Dr. Korsch who had the idea, a long time before it mattered what country had it, of organizing annual conventions, thus giving astrologers an opportunity to get acquainted, to present their views and their ideas, and, indirectly to intensify their researches into them.

Encouraged by the success of this initiative, Dr. Korsch conceived the project in 1932 of convoking the **First International Astrological Convention** at Wiesbaden. I did not have the leisure to take part in it, but the Institute delegated one of its founding members, Miss Baert of Antwerp, whose name I have already mentioned, to do so. She had to sacrifice a portion of her vacation to participate in it as the Belgian delegate. She sent us some reports about it, full of praise, that informed us of the size and quality of the German movement; and that acted as a stimulant to us.

In 1935, on the occasion of the World's Fair at Brussels, the chance presented itself for the Institute to organize an international convention in its own turn. Frankly speaking, I did not have entire faith in the success of such an enterprise, taking into consideration that it would embrace a lot of difficulties of a strictly material nature that it would be necessary to overcome one by one. Now, I have already mentioned that I lack some of the "mundane," diplomatic, and coldly realistic qualities that are indispensable to bring something of this sort into being. Besides, at that time, I scarcely had any co-workers, and I also hesitated to delegate any tasks, always with the fear that they would be viewed as forced labor. One will easily recognize in this once more the influence of Saturn dominated by Neptune. Hence, I took the organization of that convention entirely upon my self, and understandably at the price of great labor. After a lapse of ten years I ought to smile at that, in spite of all the "inferiority complex" that derived perhaps very simply from a remnant of vital deficiency. I am giving these details to explain why that convention did not make use of an Organization Committee or some similar group as is customary. That had been the difficult thing, moreover, since the idea of this convention had encountered only a rather restrained reception, and due to this its organization had been noticeably delayed. But in actual fact, my system of organization offered an unquestionable advantage: that of permitting an immediate solution, and in the best sense, of every complication or unforeseen difficulty.

The success of the **International Convention of Brussels**, which was held from the 15th to the 20th of July, 1935, surpassed by far everything that I had been able to hope for. I take note again, among the names of some hundred astrologers who participated in the event, of those of Col. Maillaud, A. Boudineau, H. Gouchon, M. Privat, and E. Symours of France; H. Korsch of Germany; P. J. Harwood, W. Tucker, and Duncan Mac Naughton of England;[29] K. E. Krafft of Switzerland; Miss Keller of Holland; E. Hentges of the Grand Duchy of Luxembourg; M. Damiani of Italy; and Mr. and Mrs. R. De Luce of the United States.

After a visit to the Planetarium of the Exposition and to the astronomical clock of Master L. Zimmer, who conferred an especial enhancement on the program, the attendees were received at the Royal Observatory of Uccle and shown about in the most agreeable fashion by its director, Mr. A. Delaporte, a discoverer of planets[30] and an astronomer of world-wide reputation, along with some of his fellow workers. In the course of other meetings, twenty-one communiqués were presented. It is known that the texts of these, as well as a history of the convention, were the subject of a special brochure published by the periodical *Demain*, of which there still remain—those interested, take note!—some copies are available.

To complement the convention there was also a dinner at one of the most picturesque restaurants of "Old Brussels," that quarter of the Exposition that carried us back a hundred years. Good humor reigned there from beginning to end; I recall with fondness the menu of that dinner, which comprised, among other dishes, a "Venusian Soup," a "Chicken Jupiter," a Stellar Bombe," and a "Stratospheric Coffee," that received everyone's vote of approval. What a small thing it takes, sometimes, to make us view life as being rosy!

No less rapturous was the reception improvised in our honor at the Pavilion of the **Union of the Belgian Periodical Press**. Its deputy administrator, namely Mr. Sluse, with his legendary joviality and dynamism, won the hearts of all the attendees. Fifty of us crowded into a little room designed to contain only a dozen people; we stayed there for a couple of hours, which revived the memories of the most sensational student gatherings of our youth.

---

[29] Translator's Note. Better known to most astrologers under his pseudonym, Maurice Wemyss; he was the author of the five volume series *The Wheel of Life*.

[30] Translator's Note. Not planets, but rather planetoids (asteroids), of which Delaporte had discovered 51.

I was about to forget—since it was not on the program—a visit to the Lion of Waterloo. There was nothing astrological in that walk, unless it was the homage implicitly rendered to the noble animal that personifies the fifth sign of the zodiac! An amusing incident took place at the top of the hill: Mr. Tucker, an English visitor, turned unexpectedly towards Miss Moulièras, Col. Maillaud's secretary and a very characteristic representative of French exuberance pushed to the maximum, and said to her point-blank with the gravest air that he could assume, "Here, Mademoiselle, we are enemies!" Needless to say, this remark produced a general burst of laughter!

The Convention ended with votes on a certain number of resolutions that were communicated to the press, which gave the public to understand that a serious movement had started up in Belgium in favor of an astrology that was scientific and practiced seriously. In particular, it was also decided that a new International Convention would be held at Paris on the occasion of the 1937 Exposition. The Astrological Society of France had also voted to establish a provisory committee to study and prepare for the creation of an International Federation of Astrological Societies of the entire world.

Unhappily, this provisory committee, at least to my knowledge, was never formed, so that resolution had no practical result.

The following year, 1936, a second Convention of Belgian astrologers was held at Brussels on the 27th and 28th of June under the auspices of the **Institute**. It closed with the establishment of a **Belgian Federation of Scientific Astrologers**, divided into three groups of members: (1) student members and members sympathetic to astrology; (2) members in possession of the necessary capabilities; and (3) members who were experts, having been in practice more than ten years, or those who were following an approved line of specialization. The Assembly of attendees admitted the following persons to the latter category: Miss Verhulst, Messrs Ch. de Herbais de Thun, Th. Chapellier, G. Antarès, Heyligers, and your servant.

Mr. Heyligers, whose name I have not yet mentioned, was the director at Liége, along with Mr. Paul Muysers of the periodical *Herschel*, whose success increased from one issue to the next, but which in spite of everything had to lower its flag at the end.

Many meetings were held by the Committee of expert members to put together the new organizational by-laws. Little by little, its structure became clear. However, being at that moment extraordinarily overloaded, and fearing to have to delay the final agreement on the regulations of the Federation in spite of myself, I entrusted that work to Mr. Chapellier, who offered his services to make up for my absence. But the remedy was worse than the sickness; for—Mr. Chapellier will not take me to task for revealing the matter!—unhappily, I intended to have more to say about the document in question, but, other problems arising, I myself lost sight of the thing. Besides, no one ever dreamed of reminding me, with the result that the **Belgian Federation** was never definitively organized. Without doubt, we had anticipated the course of the stars!

If Mr. Chapellier did wrong, I was certainly, in that instance, also culpable due to my negligence, but it should be admitted that the interest of the Belgian astrologers in such a Federation was slight and even somewhat artificial. Such initiatives in fact were only supported by the enthusiasm of one or more devotees. But they were going to be required for some more immediate tasks, and one sees the general interest weakening, and even disappearing. That is what happened there! The idea was only revived later, in 1943. Would it come to a head that time? It was very unlikely! The period scarcely seemed any more happy; it was necessary to recognize too many material difficulties—to which some divergences of views were going to be added—distracting the attention of the Belgian astrologers.

I had besides been momentarily deterred from the organization of the **Belgian Federation** by the announcement of the **Third International Convention** to which Dr. Korsch invited the astrologers of the whole world. That Convention was to be held at Düsseldorf, from the 1st to the 7th of September 1936. Aside from the interest that that reunion presented in itself, reasons of confraternity commanded me imperiously to take part in it. I represented the Belgian movement there to the best of my ability.

That Convention revealed itself to be an impeccable organization and one moreover that was honored by the participation of the official authorities. Chancellor Hitler himself made the gesture of sending a telegram of welcome, an action that made a great noise at that time. Seventeen countries were represented there, and the number of communiqués was increased in proportion; their quality was distinctly remarkable. We had a visit to the Düsseldorf Planetarium, and a one day's excursion to Koenigswinter, to Siebengebirge, and to the famous Drachenfels.[31] During the course of the Convention, we were able to be present at an examination for admission to the official title of astrologer; a delegate from the Government took part in the test. Four candidates presented themselves; but only one of the four was approved; two of the others were placed under observation; and the fourth failed. These details give some idea of the difficulty of the test.

May I be permitted here to pay justice to a truly inept proposal, but one which, in view of the author's personality, benefited from a certain amount of publicity. Germany was going to proceed with a purge among the astrologers and the occultists, ferreting out the charlatans and only sparing those who gave proof of an indisputable competence and a perfect respectability. The "professors," the "fakirs," etc. would then be ruthlessly prevented from doing any harm. In return, the Government intended to intervene officially by its recognition of the title of astrologer.

Nothing more was necessary for the French professor Laberenne to have proclaimed on one fine day that "astrology has become a Fascist science"! Doubtless, the telegram from Chancellor Hitler and the numerous French participants in the Düsseldorf Convention had terrified that brave professor, who had become

---

[31] Translator's Note. These are well-known tourist attractions along the Rhine River SSE of Bonn. The Drachenfels or 'Dragon Rock' is said to be the scene of the slaying of the dragon by Siegfried.

more of a politician than a man of science! Assuredly, one writes history as one can, but it is hardly proper to apply to a science the proceedings that are customary in a certain kitchen. I should be permitted then to take the statement of professor Laberenne as a complete incongruity, unworthy of a man of his position.

I know that today, with the spirit of exclusiveness, of intolerance, and rank prejudice that has been implanted in all spheres of thought, there are some spirits shrill in reproaching us for our contacts with the Nazi régime—since it was the one after all that was then ruling Germany.

To these shrill spirits—who no doubt see more easily the straw in their neighbor's eye than the beam in their own—I would remark that our error—if there was any—was shared by the representatives of seventeen countries, and that in order to judge certain facts, **it is indispensable to place them in the atmosphere of the epoch**. Besides, in 1937, international affairs were still not damaged to such a point that suspicion was the rule. Besides, if there is any domain from which such exclusives ought to be banished, it is surely science! And the photograph in which Dr. Korsch, Col. Maillaud, and I are shown arm-in-arm is very characteristic of the kind of spirit in vogue among astrologers at that epoch. It must not be forgotten that at that Convention we were going to try to lay the base for an **International Federation** and that in those circumstances we were very much more disposed to mutual confidence than to mistrust.

Besides, one should take proper note of the prestige that Germany had acquired in our eyes from the fact that it had recognized and organized the astrological profession, while the other countries were displaying a perfect indifference to our efforts. Doubtless, the intentions of the German Government were not so pure as we supposed then; but once more, it is necessary to go back to the atmosphere of that epoch if one wishes to judge things and people soundly.

As for that which particularly concerned the Belgian astrologers, I should also call attention to an action that occurred at the foundation of the **Belgian Federation** in 1936, one which had a strong impact on our behavior vis-á-vis the German organization.

When the conditions for admission to the category of expert members was being discussed at that Convention, one of those present, Mr. R. Bauwens, who had almost always displayed narrow and restrictive views—that were, in any case, hardly practical—contested the right of certain astrologers to elevate themselves to that category. It should be said in passing that there was no question of this being approved, since those members who had been elected to that status held it by a special and appointive vote of the Assembly. But Mr. Bauwens was of the opinion that those astrologers desirous of being recognized as expert members of the Federation should have been obliged to submit to some kind of examination before a jury composed of men of science. Naturally, the reply to Mr. Bauwens was that such a jury, whatever its value from an "official" point of view might be, could not enjoy any authority in matters concerning astrology, since it was ignorant of even the first rudiments of the science. But with Mr. Bauwens, remaining obstinate, not wanting to listen, and continuing to proscribe the Belgian Federation under its proposed form, I thought that I could suggest to him that he submit himself to the authority of an Examining Commission, such as that which was functioning at Düsseldorf, and which seemed to offer every guarantee from the point of view of competence. Consequently I decided to have personal recourse to the verdict of that commission, in such a fashion, that among the expert astrologers named to that title by the Assembly on the basis of their work and their experience, at least one would be found whose competence was affirmed by an official diploma. Moreover, that was a disguised invitation to Mr. Bauwens to render also incontestable the authority of which he seemed to approve vis-a-vis his Belgian colleagues; but Mr. Bauwens did not understand it that way, or he did not want to understand it; and, although alone in his opinion, he continued to be opposed to the works of the Federation. His only satisfaction would be to be able to say to himself that our efforts were expended to no purpose.

It cannot be said that Mr. Bauwens disdained or misunderstood the increase of prestige that a license of German origin could afford him! He was in fact present at the Düsseldorf International Convention, and if I am to believe a letter that Dr. Korsch wrote to me a little later, he strove even by some rather equivocal maneuvers in the latter's opinion, to replace me as the representative of Belgium in the International Federation. He even solicited Dr. Korsch to award him the official diploma on the simple credit of his personal fame, without his having been obliged to pass the exam!! Dr. Korsch quite understandably foiled that inappropriate request! How many toys seemed thus to be at one moment worthy of coveting, and then, circumstances having changed, lost all the charms with which one had once adorned them! Let Mr. Bauwens console himself; if he had been named the delegate from Belgium at Düsseldorf, he would perhaps be playing the role of scapegoat today in my place!

It is without doubt not superfluous to relate little actions of this sort; they clarify for a curious day the little history of the astrological movement. I will also make allusion further on to some other analogous incidents that marked the Paris Convention of 1937, where one felt an indefinable mistrust vis-á-vis some representatives of the German astrological movement. But meanwhile I shall recall again, because they belong in this chapter, two small incidents that particularly struck me during the course of my stay at Düsseldorf.

At first we were received everywhere with perfect cordiality—this was indeed good propaganda!; and the hospitality that was extended to us appeared to be very generous. Many of the French attendees of a particularly independent nature caused trouble in certain quarters and in certain department stores at Düsseldorf that were accustomed to a more formal criticism, by their dynamic fault-finding. No one, however, thought of regarding them crossly; the inhabitants limited themselves to looking at them with an amused, or at most, an astonished curiosity. The sole result was that at the end of twenty-four hours all Düsseldorf knew of the existence of the astrological Convention and the presence of a French delegation! Really, on the occasion of our reception there, Germany did not belie its old reputation of urbanity, of *Gemütlichkeit*. Besides, Dr. Korsch received us at his own home, and there were many of us to assist in the transport of likeable and powdery bottles from his cellar to his apartment. That afternoon, the international amity mounted to its highest degree, and even some flirtations, some rivalries, and some pathetic jealousies were seen to be sketched out under its influence! But I am coming now to the two incidents of which I spoke above.

In the course of the excursion of the attendees to Koenigswinter, we arrive at a certain moment before the ruins of a castle that dominated the Rhine, and at the foot of which were lined up some cannons captured from the French armies during the course of the War of 1870. On one of these cannons one could read the motto: "Si vis pacem, para bellum"[32]—If you want peace, prepare for war!"—Dr. Korsch, in the speech that he improvised when halted at that spot, made allusion to that motto, an allusion, moreover, without any malignity, and which I believe, passed unnoticed in the cordial ambiance that existed.

As I was going back down the side of the mountain a few moments later, I found myself rejoined by the Vice-president of the Convention, the painter Lantzsch-Nötzel, who posed me the following question point-blank:

—I hope that you were not hurt by the words of our President?

—Hurt? I don't know to what you are alluding! I replied, however, in all sincerity.

—So much the better! exclaimed my interlocutor, I was afraid that the allusion of Dr. Korsch to the motto inscribed on the cannons up there had bothered you! We were adversaries in 1914-1918: those things ought to be forgotten and not made the object of untimely recollection. And, if those words have injured

---

[32] Translator's Note. A saying of the Roman military writer Vegetius (4th century) in his *De Re Militari*.

you, I would ask the President to apologize to you!

It seemed to me that that was a chivalrous attitude, and one that assuredly arose from scruples not often met with; also, the incident was worth being reported. And here is the other incident which perhaps threw a certain light on the behavior of the Germans.

In the train, on our return from Koenigswinter, I was discussing with a German attendee some circumstances that led in a new course to armaments, in forecast of a new war between her country and France. I had been advised to be discreet in discussing things in that domain, the Gestapo having its ears everywhere. Besides, being desirous of not wounding in any way the national sentiments of my interlocutor, I simply wanted to convey to her that that course of armaments would constitute a regrettable vicious circle of actions, deriving perhaps from a simple misunderstanding.

—France doubtless fears the German rearmament, I said to her, she arms herself in consequence, and, without doubt, Germany also takes some precautions, perhaps also fearing France.

The reply came, immediate and plain as a pistol-shot; and my fellow passenger, until then affable and charming, grew stiff suddenly and said to me:

—Germany, Mr. Brahy, fears no one!

That was all, but that was enough! The charm was broken! My lady interlocutor turned away and thereafter watched the countryside pass by outside the train window! I also had to turn my curiosity towards some of the other attendees.

From which I concluded that Germany is by itself of an open and agreeable, even obliging, nature, but that it shows itself to be extremely touchy on the question of nationalism!

So long as it was only a question of the science of astrology, so long as one kept himself from diverting the conversation into international politics, our hosts showed themselves full of regards and perfectly indulgent. Still, I would have said that all the Germans would certainly not have demonstrated the same narrowness of spirit as the lady mentioned above; the example before that proves it. Nevertheless, this little incident seemed to me to be significant and very revealing of the state of mind of a people.

I found, however, during the course of exchanging analogous views with numerous persons, that no one replied to me in so military a fashion. All of them indeed hoped that the state of peace would maintain itself among those nations that at that time were again intent upon destroying themselves. But all of them complained of the humiliating and dishonorable lot that the Allied occupation—especially the black troops—had brought them. I would add that in general they showed themselves to be understanding of the unjust destiny that had struck Belgium during the course of the torment of 1914.

But politics constituting the least of my cares, I found our hosts at the Düsseldorf Convention as friendly as old enemies could be; and I repeat that it was necessary to believe that at that moment at the very least that opinion was shared by all the astrologers, French as well as foreigners. If this had not been so, how could one explain that they accepted the idea proposed by Dr. Korsch to found an **International Federation of Scientific Astrologers** at Düsseldorf?

Dr. Korsch, either because he was unaware of the decisions taken at the Brussels Convention of 1935 after his departure, or probably because he had stated that the project of the Federation voted then had not had any continuation, that project relating besides to a Federation of **societies**, had had in view the creation of an international association of astrologers, then of unaffiliated individuals. Besides, no one made any objection to that understanding of it, and Dr. Korsch's proposal was the object of a favorable vote given unanimously by the attendees. A working committee was immediately named; it was comprised of delegates of the countries officially represented, one delegate for each country. The designated members were these: for France, Col. Maillaud; for Holland, Miss Keller; for Switzerland, K. E. Krafft; for the Grand Duchy of Luxembourg, E. Hentges; for the United States,

R. De Luce; for Germany, Dr. Korsch; and I myself for Belgium.

It was agreed that the headquarters location of the Federation would be fixed, **until further orders**, at Düsseldorf, and that the Presidency would be provisionally entrusted to Dr. Korsch. These two decisions were taken by **unanimous voice vote**.

Let it be said in passing, I knew Dr. Korsch sufficiently well to be convinced that he would have fully agreed, at the end of a certain period of time, that another delegate should take his place as President, and that the headquarters of the Federation should be transferred to another country. At one time the question had even been raised of choosing a neutral country for that purpose—Belgium, Switzerland, or Holland. But in this sort of question chauvinism is unfortunately a governing factor to a very high degree; and, lacking a sufficient unanimity, they rallied willingly in the same proportion to Dr. Korsch's proposal that it should have a provisional character, and that in the meantime its acceptance represented a mark of deference for its author that was quite natural.

The **Third International Convention** closed then with an optimistic and essentially constructive ambience. A great hope seemed to rise for the future of the world astrological movement, truly indeed, we might be able to believe that we had attained the end that we had pursued so much, that of an international entente. However, mindful of our experience in the Brussels Convention, I maintained a certain skepticism in spite of myself; and it was in that spirit that, giving my account of the Düsseldorf Convention in the periodical *Demain*, I gave this rallying cry in favor of cooperation:

> "We must now make an appeal to the good will of everyone, so that this fine realization can develop normally. Everything must be effaced in order to attain this end: personalities, theories, conflicts of opinion, and petty egotistical considerations. Astrologers must render themselves worthy of the cause that they serve!"

I am certain that good will was not lacking; most of the astrologers were even prepared for those concessions that sooner or later would be required in the general interest of the movement. Why, after that did that great outburst of confraternity lamentably prove to be abortive? I believe I can say that the fault was due to certain political intrigues that can be understood better if one recalls the state of mind in which the sightless democracies were living at that moment. Everything that was coming out of Germany and Italy was in fact dishonorable, shot full of prohibitions, and tainted with an inhibitory defect.[33] I readily admit that that mentality had been able to reign within its political spheres; but that some scientific circles, or those calling themselves scientific, would have let themselves be afflicted by these same blinders, these same rank prejudices, that is what I have never understood and doubtless I never will understand!

---

[33] Translator's Note. I suppose this is a reference to the loud and strident propaganda blasts continually emitted by the German and Italian governments.

A Trip to the United States
The Phantom of Mrs. Elizabeth

Meanwhile, at the Revue *Demain* at the beginning of the year 1937, we received an invitation to participate in an International Convention that was to be held in New York City from the 12th to the 17th of the following May. The man who inspired this event was Mr. Ziegler, an astrologer of Miami, Florida, who revealed himself at the outset as an organizer trained in the methods of American publicity. Had he not in fact invited President Roosevelt to enhance the Convention by his presence? Had he not promised, by way of a spectacular attraction, the presence of a dozen American beauties at that Convention, all of them astrologers and very respectable too? In America, as everyone knows, women are the center of gravity of every important event; and the most serious processions there are preceded by girls in bathing suits as if it were only a matter of a common road-show!

My first inclination on receiving that invitation was to file it away without taking any action. However, it was a good opportunity to meet the principal representatives of the American astrological movement on their home grounds! But to do that would have required the dedication of four or five weeks of leisure, a thing that for many years had been impossible for me. Besides, a fairly heavy expenditure could be foreseen; and one did not easily envisage disbursements of that sort that ran the risk of seriously unbalancing my budget.

Nevertheless, the idea of participating in that Convention worked on me cunningly! Little by little, I got used to the concept of a vacation that would in some way have the character of a scientific mission. I would also say to myself that a trip of that kind would constitute a singular break, after years of incessant labor.

I was surprised one day to learn that my colleagues on the Council of the Society had made some similar reflections on their own, but in another sense. They, and in particular Mr. de Herbais, thought that the periodical *Demain*, having been given the interest that it had succeeded in polarizing around itself, could not remain indifferent to an event of this kind, and that it absolutely had an obligation to publish a report on that Convention, along with some useful considerations on the American astrological movement. But there was still the problem of the cost of the trip to think about, which was not a simple matter for a small enterprise such as ours, with minimum capital and without any financial reserves, and which had no ambition other than to cover its annual budget as adequately as possible.

It was taken into consideration that when I had founded the "Société des Éditions de la Revue Demain," the assets that I had furnished had been very reasonably evaluated. Taking this fact into account, it was finally decided—heroically indeed!—to offer me a contractual credit covering the very minimum of expenses, and to have confidence in the results of the trip, which might open up some unexpected perspectives. For me, as for my colleagues, America at that time did in fact still represent a kind of land of miracles from which the improbable itself could rise up. It was then that an idea came to me, an idea that had, in my mind, to put all the trump-cards on my side and to satisfy at a single blow all my aspirations.

I had always thought, when considering my natal stars, that sooner or later my destiny would lead me to make a great sea voyage; Neptune in the IX sector and trine the eastern horizon seemed to me to be an indication of that. Besides, I had written in my book *Contribution à l'étude de l'Astro-dynamique*, a definite statement that California could constitute the end-point of that trip, which at the time I wrote it seemed to me highly unlikely. In fact, I mistrusted myself for the principle of the planet Neptune, the inexhaustible repository of illusions and phobias; and, by my natural disposition, I was not accustomed to build castles in Spain! Such a long trip had always appeared to me as very unlikely, even inconceivable.

And here it was that the possibility of realizing such a trip was presenting itself to me! I have in fact mentioned above the particularly cordial state of my relations with the Rosicrucian Association of Oceanside; I burned with a desire finally to make the acquaintance of those distant friends, and to visit their Center of astrology and occultism.

And I said to myself that if it was truly necessary for me to cross the Atlantic,—an opportunity that normally presents itself only once in a lifetime—it would perhaps be better to make the best use of this opportunity to get the maximum satisfaction and experience from it. By means of a longer absence and a supplementary financial sacrifice on my part, it would then be possible to visit the whole United States, not only from the point of view of a tourist, but furthermore and especially from the point of view of obtaining an astrological documentation.

I also reflected that, all other opportunities aside, this transatlantic voyage would perhaps even furnish me the opportunity to make some interesting reporting. Who knows? The publication of a book might come from it, a book whose eventual success might compensate in part the expenses incurred both by the Society and by myself.

One knows now that on this point my intuition had not deceived me, since it was that trip that led me to publish *En Touriste aux Etats-Unis*, which had the most happy results both for the Éditions de la Revue Demain and for myself. Since the publication of that book, I have in fact not ceased to receive tokens of the most lively interest on the part of new readers.

However, I did nourish some apprehension as to the reception that my wife would have for my trip beyond the Atlantic; an absence of two months is not likely to be accepted with heartfelt joy, and it would have been proper for her to have been opposed to the idea of so long a separation. But I am pleased to say that she had a perfect understanding of my project and the ends I had in mind. She accustomed herself with a meritorious resignation to the prospect of my departure, knowing very well besides that there was no possibility of my taking her along on a trip that was as long, as burdened, as "dynamic" as the one that I had in mind.

The organization of that trip revealed itself to be in fact a veritable tour de force. It was necessary in the preceding interval of seven or eight weeks, and at the same time with a limited budget, to put together an itinerary that would permit me to be present for the entire length of the Convention at New York and to visit the principal centers of attraction of the United States, at the same time allowing myself a sufficiently long stay in each city to permit me to make the indispensable visits, from the point of view both of a tourist and a professional.

I finally decided to depart from Antwerp-Harwich, to visit London briefly, then to embark for Canada at Liverpool. My ship, the "Duchess of Richmond," a reputable steamer of the Canadian Pacific Line, would dock in Ireland and in Scotland before landing me in Québec. From there I would take the train to Montréal, then to New York, where I would arrive on the eve of the Convention. When that was over, I would take myself successively to Niagara Falls, to Chicago, to the Grand Canyon of the Colorado, to Los Angeles, and to Oceanside; afterwards, following a tour of California by way of Santa Barbara, Del Monte, and the Yosemite National Park, I would arrive at San Francisco. And finally, from there I would get on the train to return by way of Salt Lake City, the famous city of the Mormons, Kansas City, Saint Louis, Washington, and New York, from where I would embark on the "Queen Mary" to Cherbourg and Brussels, via Paris.

This schedule, thanks to the travel agency that had put it together, evolved without the least impediment and with the maximum of comfort and efficiency. If here and there I met with some disillusions, they were due to my own preconceived ideas or to insufficient documentation.

Also, anxious to avoid such disillusionments for those of my compatriots who might one day attempt the same trip in the land of the dollar, I promised myself that if I ever published an account of it, I would show America as it is, that is to say, what is necessary to see in it and what is not necessary. Thus there sprang up in my mind the idea of writing, as a result of my trip, a kind of romantic Baedeker, which, while documenting for the tourist the precise way to do things, would at the same time avoid the customary dryness of form of that kind of book.

I did not doubt then that the experience so acquired would permit me to undertake, two or more years later, on the occasion of the World's Fair of New York, a new trip to the United States, and to act as guide on that occasion to a group of twenty-five persons! And so the two extremes of the transatlantic voyage, the individual travel and the travel in a group, would be revealed to me with their advantages and their inconveniences.

My return on that second trip was made just in time; some days later Germany declared war on Poland!

I have recorded my impressions as a tourist at length—such as I experienced and lived them—in my book *En Touriste aux Etats-Unis*. My readers have wanted to say to me or to write to me, with a unanimity that has deeply touched me and even flattered me, that they had been so impressed, on pursuing my account, as to want to make the trip themselves. I claim to be a pretty good observer and one able to catch often at a glance the essential point of a spectacle or an incident; but in addition, my sensitivity helps me very much to record the living and moving side of things. Without doubt, I owe to these qualities my having succeeded in conveying the interest of my trip! In fact, it is simply a matter of opening one's eyes and taking an interest in everything.

And then it is necessary to say that I have "dressed up" with a rather amusing intrigue this account, which otherwise would have been, in spite of everything I have said, only a succession of rather dry notations. And I have the impression that my readers have appreciated quite as much the account of my adventures with Mrs. Elizabeth as my account of the American continent. Sometimes they do not fail to ask me, with a knowing look:

"And how about Mrs. Elizabeth? What really happened?"

Should I pretend here, for the safeguard of my good reputation and for the tranquility of my household, that Mrs. Elizabeth never existed? Or should I rather, with a care for publicity, let stand the legend that has been created around this intrigue, and which contains nothing displeasing to the self-love of an author? It is in any case very flattering for me to state that my readers add faith, even in the smallest details, to an account that they take to be an autobiography from A to Z. Do I dare to let it be known that Mrs. Elizabeth, without being entirely a myth, could well resemble in a unique silhouette two or three fugitive shapes that divide among themselves the ideal representation that I have created for myself from them? And then, Mrs. Elizabeth, was she entirely an American? So many enigmas, of which I have not furnished the solution! But can I admit here that the final episode of my book, on the eve of my departure, was really lived. Some of my readers consider it to be unlikely, and yet it is perhaps the truest of all!

But let us return to the subject of my trip and to the New York Convention. It was held in a modest "sky-scraper" of forty floors, the "New Yorker Hotel," a marvelous caravanserai for business men. They had reserved a room for me on the 34th floor; I was then "in the neighborhood." The sessions were held in the morning, in the afternoon, and in the evening. As for the lectures, they were very varied, some strictly technical or scientific, others exclusively moral or philosophical. I was obliged to select from the program those lectures that interested me and those in which I could without any inconvenience excuse myself from being present. That permitted me to visit a little of New York, which would otherwise have been impossible for me. But that did not happen without some picturesque incidents, and I will permit myself to relate some of them because they are typical of the American mentality.

Now then, Mr. Ziegler, President of the Convention, whose tact and savoir-faire I have already mentioned, did not hesitate to throw into relief at every opportunity the interest that had given birth to his initiative and the success that it had encountered. It must indeed be recognized that he had done a very good job. As I found myself to be the only European astrologer who had made the trip, my presence there no doubt conferred a special prestige on the organizer of that assembly of astrologers. Indeed on several occasions Mr. Ziegler took pleasure in pointing out that not only had some astrologers from the Western United States traveled more than 5000 kilometers to take part in the Convention, but that there was in the hall a European astrologer who had crossed the Atlantic to do so! And to give his words the support of a noisy demonstration, Mr. Ziegler would then end his speech with this appeal:

—Where are you, Gustave-Lambert Brahy; stand up, so that we can see you!

The first time this happened, I was astonished and frankly annoyed to be offered up as an object of curiosity—even though sympathetically—to the audience. The second time, I found it irritating. The third time . . . the third time I was gone, rambling through the curiosities of New York . . . and the pathetic appeal of the president fell on emptiness, the intended publicity effect lamentably missing fire. Mr. Ziegler, I think, appeared to be quite vexed! But thereafter I was left in peace!

Another day, at the stroke of noon, some of the other attendees and I left to visit the New York Planetarium. By what mischance did we run astray to the Women's Prison in Greenwich Village? I have never understood it. In my book I have told about the visit to that establishment, which seemed to me to have only the name of "penitentiary," and which showed me one of the most disconcerting aspects of the American mentality—from the point of view of a

European, that is! We had not yet dined; my stomach was crying hunger! We left there around three o'clock and went to eat in a neighboring restaurant. I was, I admit, quite embarrassed, and my perplexity must have shown on my face. Nevertheless, I did not regret this inexplicable change in the program.

One of the attendees, who was at the same time a caricaturist, Mr. Howard Duff, made everyone happy by putting on a blackboard some silhouettes of planetary types. It was Napoleon who said that a sketch was more eloquent for him than a long report. In fact, the divergences of the influences leaped to the eyes and engraved themselves on the memory better than the longest and most minute descriptions could have done.[34] I have religiously preserved as a souvenir of a breakfast given by Mr. Ziegler at the New Yorker Hotel a magnificent menu, decorated with the numerous signatures of astrologers present at the Convention and some sketches by Mr. Howard Duff. He created for himself an impression of having a pleasing good nature, which was well within the note of greeting that I found there.

To cite the names of all the attendees whose acquaintance I made in New York would assuredly be tedious; all tastes, all opinions were represented; there was even among them an authentic delegate of the Negro race who was not the least interesting of all those present, and the ten beauties promised by Mr. Ziegler were really there! I quickly made friends with Ernest Grant, the Vice-President of the Convention, who invited me to visit Washington in his company on my return from California, I also made the acquaintance of Walter Bruknus, a particularly gifted astrologer who had taken a special interest in the stock market and whose conversation was of intense interest. It was he, who, on the day of my embarking for Europe, almost made me miss the boat and brought me one of the strongest emotions of my life. It was he

---

[34] Translator's Note. Howard M. Duff, FAFA, a charter member of the American Federation of Astrologers, who always entertained the members at its biennial conventions with his sketches. Some of his sketches are reproduced in his booklet, *Astrological Types,* available from the AFA. He also designed the official seal of the AFA.

again who wrote to me at the end of 1940[35]: "I see in the chart for the declaration of war that the Maginot Line will be pierced and Paris occupied. If you have any papers to put in a safe place, do it while there is still time!" One sees from this fact that I was not dealing with an amateur astrologer!

But one of the attendees who turned out to be one of the friendliest towards me was Elizabeth Aldrich, the founder of the *New York Astrologer*, today vanished from the scene, and which brought to its director the loss of a considerable sum of money. Elizabeth Aldrich introduced me to many Astrological Centers and to a number of astrologers, in particular Mrs. Ellen McCaffery and Messrs Harold Mann and Manly Hall, three remarkable representatives of the American movement, not to mention Paul Clancy, the director of *American Astrology*, one of the most important periodicals of its kind in the United States. The opportunities to meet people were so numerous besides that sometimes I did not know which way to turn. One makes acquaintance very quickly in the United States.

It was on the Pacific coast at Los Angeles that I found again another nursery of astrologers, and one so important that it caught me totally unaware. I had an opportunity to visit Llewellyn George, director of the *Astrological Quarterly Journal* and the author of many educational books. Very communicative, he received me, not with open arms, but—if I dare to speak thus—with clenched fists, with friendly blustery forces, but five minutes sufficed to make of us the best friends in the world. When he learned that that same afternoon I was to meet James Mars Langham, a specialist in financial questions, he took pity on my ingenuousness, since it was a fact that there was no street-car nor taxi able to take me there, and that I was a considerable number of miles away from there. So he took me there in his own car, giving me a chance to admire the surroundings of Santa Monica, a sea-side resort adjoining Los Angeles. Mr. Langham received us very affably, but with a rather Britannic reserve; I think that he asked me more questions than I did him. We chatted a long time; I was due at the hotel at 6:30; it was

---

[35] Translator's Note. I think Brahy meant to say "at the end of 1939."

later than 6 o'clock when we took leave of our host. Once more Llewellyn George smiled at my naiveté, when I told him of the urgency of that rendezvous; he made me to understand that I was about as far from Los Angeles as I would be from Brussels if I were in Louvain or Malines. And again, taking me in his car, he carried me as far as possible, permitting me to catch a street-car along the route and to arrive at my rendezvous only a half hour late—a delay easily excusable for a stranger, one will agree.

My best visit naturally was at Oceanside. The greeting that was given to me on the threshold of that building, which was monastic in appearance but modern and pleasing, was truly fraternal. During one whole day I became acquainted with the thousand details of the organization of the Center, and, accompanied by one or another member of the Order, I went through the streets of the magnificent park, which belongs to the Community. By a favor that I particularly appreciated, I was able to visit the Temple—a dodecagonal structure erected on a sort of promontory with a view of the Pacific in the distance—a temple dedicated to the twelve signs of the Zodiac, and in which are held the ritual assemblies of the members who have taken formal appointments with respect to the Order. Mrs. Max Heindel, the director of the Rosicrucian Movement, did me the honor of receiving me at her table and invited me to give a talk before the members of the Association. To improvise in a foreign language was not an easy thing for me; but, aided now by one person and now by another, I made my way through that adventure with honorable mention.

I left Oceanside morally strengthened, and physically rested on my numerous nights on the railroad, yet regretting my not having planned for a much less fleeting stay. Unhappily, my itinerary enchained me without mercy, and that is why it was impossible for me to visit other interesting Centers, such as **The Church of Light** and some remarkable researchers such as Dr. Cornell, author of the extraordinarily well documented *Dictionary of Medical Astrology*.

The remainder of my trip was without any notable events from a professional point of view. But from a tourist's point of view, there were some; however, I can only refer once more to my book *En Touriste aux Etats-Unis*, those of my present readers who want to get a more complete idea of what my trip was like, of the points of view and the curiosities that it enabled me to experience, and of the habits and customs that it enabled me to observe.

And so I returned to Europe towards the end of June 1937, on the eve of the opening of the Fourth International Astrological Convention, organized in Paris by the **Société astrologique de France**, from the 17th to the 24th.

The International Convention at Paris
The End of a Dream

The Paris Convention was the first important manifestation of the Societé astrologique de France [SAF], founded at the same time as our Institute in 1926, and which counted among its members the most congenial and the most competent French astrologers. That Convention appeared to be a great success, and one realized rather quickly that it had been prepared with care.

However, the organization had been slow enough about it. In order to lead the **Societé astrologique de France** to depart from its reserve and its habitual apathy, it had required the stimulant of a dissidence, of a kind of disloyal concurrence, due to the scarcely confraternal activity of a newcomer to astrology, a recruit of note, certainly because of her culture and her original views, but unhappily driven to press on, and more preoccupied with making herself personally a star than with serving the cause of the astrological movement. But the result obtained made up for all the previous hesitation: for one thing, the presence of Minister Justin Godard at the opening ceremonies gave the Convention some degree of official patronage, and besides one noticed among the those present the name of the Abbé Blanchard, who was to present a communiqué on "The Attitude of the Catholic World towards Astrology." In it the Abbé Blanchard developed the thesis that the

Church does not entirely forbid the exercise of astrology, on the condition that it does not see in it any manifestation of a blind determinism, but only a tendency, a simple impulse, to which the intelligent exercise of free-will can always provide a counterweight. It seemed to me to be difficult not to rally behind this manner of viewing the situation, since it is in conformity with what is taught by observation and experience.

The Paris Convention was therefore a remarkable success. The organization was seen to be perfect and left nothing to be desired when compared to that at Düsseldorf, only the hall in which the sessions were held aroused some criticism because of its small size and its imperfect ventilation; we experienced some almost Saharan temperatures in it. Mrs. McCaffery, the congenial New York astrologer who had been anxious to make contact with the European astrologers, complained bitterly about it, accustomed as she was to American halls in which the atmosphere is constantly purified and cooled. But the Europeans, used to less comfort, took it in their stride; and besides, the interest in the sessions would have made them endure even greater sacrifices had it been necessary.

Among the astrologers were the English, Mrs. Subbury-Hurren and R. Gleadow; Belgian, Mmes. Michaux and Verhulst, Messrs Antarés, L. Horicks, the Viscount de Herbais de Thun, and myself; Dutch, Miss Keller; German and Austrian, Lantzsch-Nötzel, Kern, Regensreif; Polish, A. Prangel; American, Mrs. McCaffery and Mr. Léonard; Italian, Mr. Damiani; Swiss, Dr. Duprat. All these had come to swell a serious assembly of French astrologers, among whom one recognized Drs. Vannier, Allendy, Brétéché, and Coton-Alvart; Messrs Kerneiz, Boudineau, Gouchon, Volguine, Lagier, Gastin, Lasson, Cognié, Pezet, Courand, Fournier, Bernoud; Mesdames Tritz, Vinal, Faery, Bucco, Lechaut, Parenty, Conte, Pascal, and Janduz; and Miss de Mouliéras. In addition, the papers that were presented were numerous and for the most part remarkable. Scientifically speaking, it is necessary to say again that the Paris Convention elevated astrology to a level rarely attained.

Unhappily, certain regrettable incidents cast a rather trouble-some note over this enthusiasm.

I have said that the Paris Convention had roused up a dissi-dence.[36] There was nothing more laudable than that certain indi-viduals had dreamed of using these conditions to reconcile "brother enemies!" But to meet this end, was it necessary to throw the program of the Convention into disorder, in order to introduce into it surreptitiously and without any kind of announcement a more or less commercial paper emanating from a dissident mem-ber of the Convention? Certainly, many properly registered atten-dees saw themselves constrained, either to place their own papers beyond the prearranged limits—and then before a reduced audi-ence—or simply to suppress them. The procedure was inelegant and in fact entirely incorrect.

But the gravest incident took place in connection with the Inter-national Federation created two years earlier at Düsseldorf. Dr. Korsch, not having obtained his passport in time—since the Ger-man police were proceeding, it seemed, with a new investigation into the subject of astrology—had only been able to arrive in Paris the day after the end of the Convention; and Mr. Lantzsch-Nötzel, who had replaced him, had reached Paris after the opening date. From that, it was only a step to maintain that the Germans who had intended to attend were no longer free to travel at their own conve-nience, and in consequence of that, that the Federation founded at Düsseldorf in 1936 would not be free of its movements if one con-firmed its existence. The organizers of the Paris Convention took that step deliberately.

Let us admit that, in order to obviate the fears and objections that could emanate from certain of those in attendance, it was pro-posed to transfer the seat of the Federation into France or some-where else! Let us further admit that if there had been some re-proaches to make to Dr. Korsch, it might rather have been sug-

---

[36] Those of my readers who are unaware of this may wish to refer to the issues of the Revue *Domain* of that epoch, where all the convincing details were reported.

gested to name someone else as president! It seemed to me that it would have been an elementary correction to permit Dr. Korsch to give an explanation—he who had worked seriously and who had even made some important advances of his own money. What reason was there to profit from the absence of Dr. Korsch with feverish and ridiculous conspiratorial attitudes in order to torpedo the International Federation? Doubtless, that flattered French chauvinism, but in addition I have good reasons to believe that, at the Assembly where the matter was discussed, the French astrologers—at least certain ones among them!—submitted passively to an idea of an entirely political order.

If one recalls the kind of spirit that was reigning then in French political circles—the words of Laberenne: "Astrology, the fascist science!"—it will be quickly understood that this hypothesis of mine is neither gratuitous nor improbable.

Besides—and here is what definitely proves the headlong haste and confusion of motives—the conclusions that were read in the name of the French delegation **were only ratified the next day by the Astrological Society of France!** Hence, they had no legal validity on the day when they were read to the Convention!

It will be acknowledged that that was done to treat the attendees in a completely off-handed manner. Also, the discussion was interrupted by sharp words and forcible interruptions.

How many times was I shocked by this chauvinism when the spirits became sharper and sharper with the foreboding of an imminent new war. But, in spite of everything, I tried to recreate some bonds of confraternity or at least of a good scientific camaraderie between the German and French astrologers.

On the German side, I was persuaded not to advance too far along that path, while on the French side I was informed that my intentions were considered to be suspect.

That reminded me of the outcry in certain circles that a few years earlier had accompanied the publication in *Demain* of an article entitled "Fascism or Democracy," of which I would not change a single word even today. In those years that preceded the great conflict, political prejudice ranted with such a blind rage that five years of suffering and misery—one can notice it even today—have not succeeded in restoring it to more reasonable proportions. Quite to the contrary, one can say that prejudice came out of the war more intractable than ever.

The Paris Convention was the last important public manifestation of the international astrological movement. In 1938, one believed that a catastrophe was going to release itself upon the world, but then there was Munich. However, the euphoria did not last long; the fever increased progressively, and, in that atmosphere of insupportable tension and distrust, how could there have been any question of a Convention or a Federation? On the contrary, in the Astrological Society of France, one witnessed a regrettable policy of exclusions and suspicions that provoked the creation of new groups and the crumbling of a movement that had begun under the best auspices. The ridiculousness of some of these decisions does not seem to have occurred to the minds of those who took the responsibility for them. Jupiter definitely blinds those whom he wishes to destroy.

But, so imperfect, so ephemeral were the actualities born of the four international assemblies whose essential traits I have rapidly sketched out here, that it is necessary to acknowledge that they have led to some remarkable results. In this connection it is necessary to judge these results, not as they might have been, but rather as they might not have been. The astrologers had worked as well as they could in accordance with their means; they certainly did as well, everything being considered, as the politicians who founded the League of Nations—producing something that was more beautiful for the symbol that it represented than for the results that it achieved.

A Critique of the Modern Astrological Movement Conflicts and Polemics

Having arrived at this point in my book, it might perhaps be asked of me, What do I think of today's astrological movement—that is, to say it in other words, what do I think of modern astrologers. It is a very delicate thing to pronounce oneself on this subject when one is an astrologer himself and when one participates in the movement in question. What is certain is that even today it is necessary to have one's faith bolted to his body in order to defend the theory of astral influences. To put it another way, can those who devote all their time to it, even those with the title of "professional," be considered as particularly courageous. One will have been able to judge all those ironies, the sarcasms, and unspoken scorn—without taking any account of the attacks and struggles, or of their source—that the Belgian movement has had to endure and undergo before asserting itself. No doubt it is somewhat the same in every enterprise. But the effort would be less great and more fruitful, and the success more rapid, if the astrologers of today were to display some of those qualities, whose lack is frequently and disastrously revealed. Those qualities, which I list here in what seems to me to be their order of importance, are objectivity, critical sense, and good fellowship.

Let us examine each of these in turn. It will be understood that if

I permit myself to make certain allusions to specific facts, I abstain from citing any names. I am not trying to make matters worse—quite the contrary!

Objectivity appears to be particularly precious and necessary when it is a question of giving out a prediction or a judgment on an occurrence, or a sequence of occurrences, on whose subject opinion is shown to be particularly touchy. The absence or deficiency of this quality is revealed as being particularly unfortunate in certain authors, whose merit or scientific value cannot be contested. For example, I wish that the numerous versions of Chancellor Hitler's horoscope that have been published, containing so many inconsistent affirmations—today plainly controverted by the facts—had not been made. How many times since 1931 did they make him fall from power and die? And that was because the Führer's personality inspired a manifest repulsion in almost everyone, indeed a kind of hatred that warped all their judgments. How many times was the same thing done in the case of Il Duce? One has seen certain astrologers—otherwise competent ones, I repeat—announce that his end is near; and then, when he persisted in living, proclaim again the imminence of a violent end a few months later? But, at the end of the year 1944, Hitler and Mussolini were still there! Even if they had to fall very soon, they had already given the lie to almost all the predictions that had been emitted on that subject.

There is also the lack of objectivity—or, what is even more unpardonable, a grave negligence, or a manifest indifference—that made them write that the ex-king Edward VIII would have a long and happy reign, that France would be victorious in 1940, and many similar predictions. The authors of these prophecies suffer a personal loss of prestige, and astrology itself has to undergo the repercussions.

As for the authors of these erroneous prognostics, however, one cannot pretend that they would all have lacked the courage necessary to express their opinion. Certainly they would have been able to have been guided by a patriotic scruple, namely to hide from the public the real judgment that had resulted from their investigations. But if certain ones of them have always been governed in their attitude by the concern of not doing anything that could be criticized by the public (but in that case, one might legitimately ask, why would they want to play at being prophets?), others have shown in different circumstances that they would not hesitate to follow an idea that the approval of the crowd had refused to support. I could cite as an example of such a state of things the granting of diplomas by the **International Federation of Scientific Astrologers**, founded in 1936 at Düsseldorf. Because of this, a French astrologer who had, however, been one of the mainsprings of the Paris Convention, saw himself excommunicated. Those are the kinds of dangers that an independence of spirit exposes itself to.

As for me, I am always spurred on by objectivity, and that has almost always led me to give out judgments or prognostics that jostle the public opinion of the moment. Without doubt I will have an opportunity to give some further typical examples. When it happened that I deceived myself—for that happens to everybody; and, of course, I make no exception in my own favor!—it is rather inexperience or inadequacy of means that is to blame. I certainly do not reproach a remarkable French researcher, but one a little too enthusiastic, for having foreseen in 1938 "fifteen years of peace in Europe"; the thesis that was presented was too new and the reference material too reduced to permit one to draw so certain a conclusion. But, that the same astrologer had presented certain theories as articles of faith and had consequently announced as pure certitudes some events on which his sentiments conferred a character that was particularly agreeable to his own eyes, and that was a lack of objectivity, a lack of moderation that one can only deplore.

Moderation! Another lacuna in many modern astrologers! And this lack of moderation makes itself singularly felt when there is a need for exercising their critical sense, whether this is with regard to the events themselves, or more simply with respect to certain works or certain theories.

It is rare that a book does not contain one or more errors. The number and the importance of these evidently conditions the judgment of the critic; but, is it necessary to condemn the entire work of an author under the pretext that only one part of it is stained with imperfections? Some years ago, a French astrologer conceived the idea, eminently praiseworthy, of editing an "Encyclopedia of Astrological Instruction."[37] Perhaps this initiative was somewhat precipitated by certain maneuvers of rejection, of which the author had to complain in another way! It is always the case that the purely mathematical and astronomical exposition of the question, and notably the calculation of the chart, permits some errors. (One knows that technical precision is not a predominant quality in the weaker sex, and that that sex feels more particularly at ease in the field of intuition.) Some condemned the entire work without noticing that the part relating to interpretation contained some excellent things. Would it not have been simply fair to have separated the good part from the bad? Fundamentally, what book is there that would be resistant to a judgment so partial and total?

Certain astrologers, joining in this lack of objectivity and also displaying a total lack of good fellowship, have even expressed their intention to condemn the entire block of everything that had been written before them. Without taking the trouble to read or even to skim through the works of those that they pretended to vilify, they called one a "smoky candle", another a "plagiarist," and so on, exhausting in that way a remarkable string of verbal insults and rash judgments.

We have seen above that without going as far, certain Belgian astrologers, who had no title to lord it over the others, have criticized their fellow astrologers at random and have condemned by one stroke of the pen everything that had been done before them. This resembles somewhat the huckster's shouts at the fair: "You

---

[37] Translator's Note. Possibly a reference to the work of the French astrologer Janduz (Jeanne Duzea), *Encyclopédie Astrologique Française* (1936).

118

are going to see what you are going to see." And generally, you see nothing at all!

Does not the most extreme astrologer of this kind push his audacity and his impertinence so far as to want to stamp his subversive theories with the seal of a pretended revelation? We are not inventing this! It is the author himself who discloses himself textually in one of his first works. He speaks out as though he had been mandated by some Great Spirit to bring to the world the Law that it had been waiting for!!! This is why one has seen him work out, as a replacement of the astrological tradition—which is nevertheless a proven basis—a set of personal views, interesting of course, but born from a very particular concept, in which occultism played a large part! It is somewhat as if a profane person, seeing things from his own point of view, made a pretence of giving advice on the works and thoughts of the masters of modern chemistry and physics, while denouncing their stupidity, their vacuity, and their nonsense, and was then astonished that a unanimous approbation had not rallied around him.

It is understood that as well disposed as one might be with regard to a fellow astrologer, it is impossible to subscribe to the extremity of such opinions.

That Ptolemy, who passes for the grand master of the astrological tradition, may have pillaged or even distorted certain ones of his predecessors, one can in a strict sense pretend, indeed even admit. But it is possible to express that idea without the use of trivial and pejorative language and without constantly having injury and scorn on the tip of one's tongue. Now, the vocabulary of the colleague of whom we are speaking is particularly nasty; the words "poison," "dusty," "evacuation," "vomitings," and other such terms come forth constantly from his pen! Evidently, it is to demonstrate by that means a very high opinion of his own talents and intelligence! The race of Alcibiades is not yet extinct, as one knows! But at least in his ambitious pursuit of notoriety, Alcibiades only cut off his dog's tail, an act that scarcely risked disturbing public order.

But that, from a preconceived opinion and with some disloyal and malicious intentions, one might want to throw down the traditional edifice of astrology in order to replace it with a jumble of confused and fantastic precepts which have—contrary thus to the tradition—undergone no proof by experience, is an assault that no careful astrologer of good renown in his science could tolerate.

I do not wish to rehearse polemics that are very nearly extinct; but one will recall that in 1937 *Demain* published a "Response to a Provocation" that made a big noise, and in which the confrere in question[38] was called upon to respect certain rules and certain realities. It was on the eve of the International Convention of Paris.

For some time, in fact, a number of French astrologers had complained of the procedures of their "confrere" and asked our periodical to intervene. To the end of attempting a rapprochement on the basis of mutual understanding, *Demain* opened its columns on the contrary to the contradictor in question, in order to permit him to present and to defend his ideas and to reply to certain objections. But that gesture only envenomed things; for the beneficiary of that favor quickly adopted a low polemical tone; he began again to maltreat and injure those who had not shown themselves to be entirely in accord with his statements, and—an action that crudely demonstrated his total bad faith—he refused to publish the replies—however moderate—that might be addressed to him on that subject. In short, he showed such disloyalty and such a low baseness in the discussion that *Demain* decided to teach him a lesson. In addition, always using the same roundabout procedures, he had just organized a dissident Convention, trying to give a wrong tone to and to divert to his own profit the publicity made for the official Convention. Once more, it was his right to want to create a movement and even a Convention of his own; but, if he had at least done

---

[38] Translator's Note. This was the French mining engineer and astrologer Pierre Victor Émile Maurice Rougie (1884-1953), who wrote under the name of 'Dom Necroman' (later, 'Dom Neroman'). He was the *enfant terrible* of French astrology. Viscount Charles de Herbais de Thun gives some additional coments on Dom Ne(c)roman in his *Encyclopédie du momement astrologique de langue française* (Brussels: Éditions de la revue Demain, 1944).

it properly, loyally, and in a measured fashion! With his culture aiding him—for that personage is undeniably cultivated!—I dare say he would have interested many people, he would perhaps have even taken the chief position in the French astrological movement.

For an animator may be pardoned for having exaggerated views, for pushing his demonstrations too far, for displaying his theories too complacently, and for assuming some things to be "personal discoveries" that had been said before him. But here an overweening vanity was mingling with a total ignorance of certain matters! One felt that not only was there an unhealthy tendency on the part of the incriminated confrere to denigrate and scorn openly the opinions and the work of others; but all the falsehoods about the self-styled new theories and the (seemingly) revolutionary ideas ended up by very nearly faithfully reconstituting the tradition. The author acknowledged it himself—thus discovering in that the proof of his own genius! After that, why all these falsehoods, one truly asks himself, unless it is to put in the limelight, without any regard to the delicacy of the means, a man who wanted willy-nilly to play the role that he believed had been predestined for him?

Besides, these falsehoods came to a head with some really frightening declarations that their author candidly recognized. It is thus, as I have just said, that he had astonished himself by having been able to reconstitute the so hated astrological tradition by means of his own deductions. It is thus that, having established a method of house division that he believed to be new, he was surprised to hear it said by one of his students (one who at least had the merit of having acquired some knowledge of the classic works on astrology) that it was in fact the theory of Campanus!!! I am not inventing any of this. It is written down in black and white by the author himself! Another time, this same individual proclaimed that to his knowledge there had never been any question of considering hours in a certain astronomical sense that he is now exposing to view. Well, these same hours called "unequal hours" were utilized by the ancient authors; and certain instruments for calculating them—astrolabes, for example—are precisely based on them.

It was, therefore, indispensable and even healthy for this author to be snubbed publicly! And he was! Perhaps that did not cure him, but he must have gotten the message in some measure! Nevertheless, it didn't prevent him from romancing astrology!

Let us recognize, however, that thanks to his culture and his original views, his articles and his books are read by many astrologers. And they are right to do so, for there is always something to glean when one accepts, even with a mistrustful eye, an unaccustomed point of view.

One more little action illustrates the outrageousness of that confrere and his frantic mania always to be the only one to be right in every matter.

Some years earlier, when he had just begun to make contact with the astrological movement, I encountered him in Paris in a well-known group to which I had been unexpectedly invited to participate in a discussion. The attendance was light, since the discussion had only been announced by word of mouth. Let it be said in passing that an amiable tone reigned in the group—everyone talking about different things, all at the same time. I finally began to speak and talked for several minutes. And while I was developing my first point, I was interrupted by this petulant confrere, who, without waiting for the end of my statement, presented me with an objection. Having disposed of that, I was preparing to resume, when he objected again, and, carried away by his own eloquence, requested permission to speak, and . . . continued the discussion himself. The President not intervening spontaneously to restore order to that Bedlam, I did not want to make an appeal to his singularly feeble authority, since it was hardly worth the trouble. And I had only to sit down again and mingle with the others, who, without paying any attention to the interrupter himself, had resumed their conversations.

If the anecdote that I have just reported makes you ready to smile, is it not regrettable that some procedures such as those that I mentioned above could not have been introduced into the astrological movement? When their cooperation is revealed to all as being singularly necessary to lead to the triumph of their ideas, too many astrologers still remain dominated by concern for their personal independence, their petty vanity, their chauvinistic or political "labels." A singular dispersion results from this, as does some strange contradictions in all of their efforts. And what inertia is encountered when an appeal is made to the spirit of confraternity—for example, in the matter of statistics or of communication and documentation!

However, let us not push severity too far! Most of the researchers must dream first of all of assuring their material life; consequently, they only have a reduced amount of leisure at their disposal to devote to their science. And it can certainly be accepted as true that they dream of treating the questions that interest them the most before those that preoccupy their confreres. But it is just there that the interest of a central organization is revealed, one that could assemble the maximum amount of data and direct the research and the inclinations. How is it that the astrologers of all countries do not understand this? Is it really necessary to admit that most of those among them do not have sufficient faith and are rather moved by a banal concern for curiosity than by strictly scientific motives.

Let us condemn even more severely the manifestations of political tendencies that have marked the most recent years of such an important society, for example the torpedoing of the *International Federation* of which I have spoken in the preceding chapter, the exclusion of certain members out of grotesque motives, etc. All of that, I repeat, makes one think that the directors of that Society were then obeying some secret passwords, and that they would only accept their incorporation into an International Federation with the strict condition that that Federation was under French jurisdiction, and probably even under some political jurisdiction?

If that was the situation, we would not wager very much on the future of the said Federation and still less on the future of the group in question.

It might perhaps be objected that these things only concern the French astrologers, and that consequently they do not concern me. I will say two things in reply to that: the first is that I am not criticizing them with a sterile intent, but indeed with a constructive intent; the second is that since I am concerned about the success of an international association, it is perfectly right for me to point out the faults and the maneuvers of those who are opposed to it. However this may be, one sees by the preceding what gaps remain to be filled before the modern astrological movement can pretend to have any complete success. And besides, it would be necessary that, being what they are, the astrologers form a front to conquer the last bastions of rank prejudice that separate them from that end. Without doubt, the adversaries of astrology are beginning to feel themselves helpless, for their attacks are being made less frequently, less perfidiously, and little by little they are losing their sharpness; their arguments, which are down at the heel today, no longer make an impression close to the last of those indifferent or profane, and the last enemies of our science. But we cannot rest on our laurels—which are too modest still—before we have completed our victory and before we have definitively imposed silence on these tardigrade detractors. And in order to do that, I say one more time, union should be imposed.

This is why, and I repeat it over and over again, it would be necessary for astrologers to have given proof of more confraternity, of more moderation, and of more objectivity. Instead, we see only those distressing consequences for astrology that have already existed – the failure of certain enthusiastic prognostics emitted with a great noise, which I have alluded to above.

At the Paris Convention in 1937, the Abbé Blanchard had thrown out some indications of a possible semi-official recognition of astrology by the Catholic Church. Certain astrologers could remain indifferent to that phase of the question—it is their right to do so; but we insist that that result was of importance all the same, and it opened up some considerable prospectives for the future of the astrological movement. Because of the lamentable prognostics in question, the initiative of the Abbé Blanchard met with compromise, he having been the first to realize that his idea of throwing a bridge across between the two theses that had been too long opposed was coming too soon. The modern astrologers were not sufficiently mature to reply to that advance. There too, the lack of an organization and of any coordination of the astrological movement was plainly apparent, and it was profoundly regrettable.

Alas, it is to be feared that the present conflict, which will have exacerbated not only nationalisms but also rank political prejudices, has seriously deferred those prospects for union that at one moment seemed so close at hand, unless from some universally endured sufferings and injustices there should rise up precisely, from the force of its evidence, the necessity for cooperation and for union in all the domains.

May the present critique at least be able to contribute to avoiding in the future a return to the errors and the misunderstandings that kept the science of astrology from being publicly recognized before that new World War!

"The Public, Such as it is."

We have said a lot about astrology. Now it is time to say a little about the public, whose mentality essentially conditions the behavior of the practitioners of astro-dynamics.

In general, the public is too naive, too credulous—that has been known for a long time. It accepts flashy affirmations too easily for authentic truths. Because of this, it is subjected to two radically opposed tendencies.

On the one hand in fact, tradesmen, who are both clever and deprived of all scruples—professors, fakirs, mages, and others pretending to similar high-sounding titles—falsely give assurance that they can, by the simple act of their revelations, transform a miserable life into a fortunate existence; they affirm that their knowledge is infallible and can do everything, even attract luck in the lottery. By excessive duplicity, they even pretend to act as philanthropists, thus assuring themselves an almost infallible means of devouring their clientele, once they have been able to seize their confidence.

The makers of series horoscopes—whose methods I have amply analyzed in some of my books[39]—have fantastically large advertising budgets and consequently reach tens of thousands of individuals—perhaps even hundreds of thousands! Their influence is then as great as it is ill-omened.

---

[39] See in particular my book, *La Mystère des Influences astrales* [The Mystery of Astral Influences].

In the face of these, the serious astrologers show themselves to be either more reserved, or less flashy, or they—and I am one of them—even proceed to present astrology as a simple science of probabilities, in which divination plays no role, and which therefore cannot predict the unfolding of events with certainty.

Personally, I have always compared astrological prognostication to a simple road-map, one that gives warning of dangerous turns, difficult climbs, troublesome stretches, etc. Everyone clearly remains free to approach the places marked out without diminishing the speed of his vehicle and without taking even minimal precautions. But if the journey ends in a crash, who must then be accused?

Here again, astrological foresight can be compared to a reconnaissance that pioneers and explorers make of an unknown country before they enter into it. When one knows that one will have to cross rivers and mountains, and at what points, when one has determined the kind of inhabitants, and the flora and fauna that is characteristic of a region, it is evident that one has put all the trump cards on his side, and that one has taken the necessary precautions in every regard.

The appearance of astrological prognostication is hardly different! If, for example, the birth chart denotes the risk of an accident, there is no absolute certainty of this, and, in any case, the fact does not necessarily make a dramatic appearance. But if such a risk has been determined to exist by a serious professional, it is to be supposed that it has been based on sufficient indices of probability; consequently, it is proper to take it into consideration. And then, there are two possibilities!

The first, absolutely negative, consists of hypnotizing oneself to this perspective, certainly a disagreeable one, and to think by what circumstances the accident could happen, what consequences it would be necessary to allow for, etc. . . .; in short, to do oneself more harm a long time in advance, and perhaps in pure loss, than the danger in question would have been able to do.

This attitude is that of a good part of the clientele, and especially of the public at large—essentially emotional and impressionable. It does not lead to any good; also, to consult astrology in this negative spirit is more harmful than truly useful.

The second attitude, which is a constructive one, is to envisage the astrologer's conclusions with courage, to say to oneself philosophically "we shall see"!, and as a precaution to take out life insurance or insurance against accidents. Thus, every serious consequence is neutralized in advance, and in this case the warning has an incontestable utility.

One sees that an astrological diagnosis must be taken in the same sense as that of a lawyer, for example, or a physician. Essentially, it consists of putting oneself on guard against the risks that you would not have suspected by yourself—to indicate to you the parade of events that are imposing themselves upon you and the precautions to take. It should have for its object that of easing the grip of responsibilities, of showing you the extent of your duties to yourself, to your family, or to your superiors, even to your inferiors. If you think about it, you can see that the scope of utilization that it presents is immense!

In my astrological contacts with the public, I have almost always had to fight to impose this state of mind; for I have had to deal as often with the impressionable public of the first category as with the thoughtful and intelligent public of the second category. It was not always without difficult that victory was achieved.

And then, another mentality which I have often enough had to contend with—the curiosity of the crowd—is generally of a hardly elevated order. For every single consultation looking toward the end of moral straightening, cultural improvement, or inclining towards spiritual considerations, I have certainly registered a hundred on the sole material subjects that preoccupy almost every human being—money and love. On these hundred solicitations, it was even necessary to count some touching on some rather equivocal problems: for example, the disappearance of a partner with whom one is not on good terms, union with a person who is not free—or who is free herself while the client is not—and so on. Problems with which an honest man is not always at ease and must sometimes show that he is not!

In general, I have done my best to respond to these curiosities without any spiritual impetus, considering first of all that a practical demonstration was a useful means of advertising, but even further that it was possible by so doing to make an advantageous modification of the public mentality with regard to astrology by means of the life problem.

That is why I have always formulated my forecasts in a constructive and thoughtful sense and not under a form that could confer upon them the air of a depressing or hopelessly fated outcome. And I have always given advice to my co-workers in the same way. I have striven ceaselessly to inculcate in them an optimism in the matter of astrological forecasts. How many times, when they had before them a natal horoscope that made them lose hope because of the absence of any benefic configuration, have I not said to them: "Interpret this chart as if it had at least 20 percent good things in it!" In fact it is always necessary to take into account that tendency that quite naturally pushes a human being to dramatize things, or to cast a shadow on prospects; one is prone to do it because of the fact that one has a natural tendency to characterize the character of a destiny as fortunate or malefic in accordance with the number of propitious or inauspicious aspects that one finds in the natal chart. But by so doing, one is neglecting two factors!

The first is the force of habit, a factor that makes unlucky events merely disconcerting to a man who is usually lucky, but disturbing to the point of pain for those whom destiny has already accustomed to a generally unhappy state of affairs; the event, then, has more than a relative importance for them and does not register on the same scale as it would in a less harsh life.

The second factor—and here it is necessary to implicate the astrological tradition, at least in the bookish form that its commentators most often give it!—is to believe that a bad aspect in a chart inevitably corresponds to some form of bad luck. Doubtless, a harmful configuration will never bring anything good with ease and stability, but it can bring about something good through a painful struggle, or in not very agreeable circumstances, or again by surrounding it with a character fraught with more or less insecurity. Under that approach, one would not know how to draw one's attention as much as it should be drawn to the texts that old Morin has left to us—that astrologer of genius.

That is why I have already looked for a way to consider the best in a natal horoscope, to present the prospects in the least disquieting way that it was possible to discover. I have never said to a client: "You will be in danger of death at such and such a time"; rather, I have said, "Take care and watch such and such an organ of the body, for, towards such and such a time, you may experience some physiological complications of a serious nature, which may even reach a real degree of seriousness if you neglect them."

That is why I have always insisted on considering before anything else the good qualities revealed by a chart, while dwelling upon the faults as little as possible. Experience demonstrates in fact that one does not combat a deficiency by a frontal attack but rather by smothering it progressively under the concerted action of positive virtues that one undertakes to reinforce ceaselessly. A particular passion, for example, can more easily be reduced in intensity by progressively encouraging the opposite quality than by striving to strangle its manifestations brutally.

All that may seem to be a matter of slight shadings! But—be well persuaded of this—there is a very distinct difference in the results of an order given in two different ways, for example: "Don't poke along!" or "Hurry up!" In the first case, the thought preserves the imprint of the words "poke along," and the will to act is not awakened. But in the second case, on the contrary, the spirit molds itself on the verb "to hurry," and it receives an impression of dynamism that pushes it to conform as soon as possible to the injunction received.

I am not unaware that that manner of prognostication is less "spectacular" than any other, and can give an impression of soothing the client. It perhaps also gives the impression of a "fuzzier" rendering. I know that certain astrologers reproach me for this tepidity because their own nature drives them to speak out categorically, to "hit the nail on the head." I think quite simply that they have not envisaged the problem from the same angle that I have. In the main, many misunderstandings arise from the fact that each one of us considers things in our own fashion and that we would not dream of always having to define clearly at the outset the object and the ends of our statements.

In sum, and it is this that is important in my eyes, I have acted as logic and my conscience commanded me to act! If I have been wrong, the consequences of that "error" are almost zero. But, if my point of view is correct, and if I had acted otherwise, my prognostics could have been responsible for some often disastrous consequences. And it is against having that responsibility that I have wanted to guarantee myself!

In my contact with public clients, I have naturally had numerous and varied experiences, some of them picturesque, sometimes frankly disagreeable, indeed even ambiguous.

Physicians are very familiar with a certain class of patients who are more or less abnormal, and who come to their consultations with the end in mind that one imagines. I have also done business with that special clientele that hangs around men of letters and who are haunted imperiously by an insatiable curiosity and a love of the romantic.

If one has succeeded in portraying in a lively manner a personage whose deportment appears to be a little chivalrous, or if one has succeeded in relating with the shiver of reality a fine love-affair or a thrilling adventure, it is not necessary for him to do anything more to make certain women believe that the author has put himself on the scene in his work, sheltered by his incognito, and has wanted to address some romantic declarations to certain of his lady readers.

Thence, the enthusiastic tenor of certain letters from female admirers, and I leave it to you to imagine all the complications that can result from it.

Really, if certain authors with few scruples abuse the sentiments that they have given rise to in that way, I certainly pity their victims; but I also believe that the lesson those victims can draw from it can only be a salutary one.

I shall not report here any case of that sort, first because such cases would hardly afford any useful instruction in themselves, and then because these are very delicate matters, even very painful sometimes, and ones on which it is not proper, under the pretext of confidences, to confer a little half-hearted seal of approval. Moreover, sensual spice is not one of the means that I employ to merit the attention of the public.

Besides, with the assistance of habit, I have learned to remain impassive, even affable, in the presence of both the petty and the grand dramas of existence: the gentleman controlled by his wife who is interested in a little girl-friend, the lady enchained by her conjugal ties who dreams of passionate adventures and romantic embraces, the rich patron who has the chart of his favorite secretary studied—and so many more that I know!

All these requests for investigation are presented, moreover, with the well marked desire to avoid being compromised openly. Some of them are introduced frankly without any hypocritical detours, by virtue of the well-known principle that boldness that rests upon an open candor often overawes the listener. The others present themselves under complicated approaches and in an atmosphere of embarrassment that attempts to save face. This little eccentricity is very amusing to observe! Evidently one does not enjoy exposing his weaknesses! Besides, it is necessary to be indulgent with things of that sort.

Certain situations on the contrary merit special interest. In some instances, at the moment of filling out the record card of a client who was named Mrs. X. . . . the following dialogue was taking place:

—Your marital state, Madam? Married, I suppose?

—No, sir; single!

—Divorced or separated perhaps?

—No, sir!

In such a case, impassiveness is the rule! It is useless to inquire why the client is calling herself "Mrs." However, one soon becomes suspicious, for the questioning continues thus:

—Children? None, naturally!

—Yes, sir! One! (or, in some cases, two).

Most often, one finds himself face to face with the sentimental drama of a stubborn and proud temperament that is not afraid to brave public opinion rather than to have recourse to the baseness and banality of abortion. But one perceives the courage that has sometimes been necessary for these worthy souls to maintain their attitude during the years!

All that, however, is the current state of affairs! It is useless to delay here any further! Nevertheless, I will tell about some cases of sufficient curiosity, that they were still able to take me by surprise, despite my long experience that had hardened me against any astonishment!

One day a lady of mature years and austere manner was shown in to my office; she seemed very ill at ease. It was plain that a very intimate question was driving her, but that her modesty was being put to a rude test. Lack of experience, no doubt!

After ten minutes of preliminaries, many changes of direction had not yet put my client on the road to confidences. I then posed the ritual question:

"May I know, Madame, what is bothering you?"

Silence! Her countenance more and more secretive. Decidedly I am faced with a singularly Saturnine client! I encourage her:

"Well, Madame—an affair of sentiment, no doubt?

A moment of hesitation, then an affirmative movement of the head! Encouraged by this first success, I persevered:

"You are no doubt married?"

This time the response is categorical:

"No, sir!"

"Then it is he who is not free?

Another silence! But an affirmative nod of the head!

"But Madame, this is an almost commonplace occurrence! There is nothing to be upset about at this point. Besides, consider me as a sort of confidant who has already understood the matter in all its facets and who assures you that in my office what goes in one ear goes out the other!

My client did not have the air of finding herself any more freed from her hesitation in spite of this eloquent exhortation! She shook her head and limited herself to saying:

"It is not so commonplace as you believe!"

I think to myself: "Good, a classic case, the occurrence that one believes happens only to oneself." But I insist:

"But see here, Madame, you are not the first woman who has fallen in love with a married man! It is an everyday occurrence!

"I have not told you, sir, that he was married!"

"No, but you have said that he was not free; it is the same thing!"

"Not necessarily!"

All of a sudden, I am embarrassed. I flounder for a moment between these two contradictory statements. I detect a charade of a new sort; but no light comes!

"Well, Madame, I'm not with you. You must explain it."

My client re-immerses herself in her initial silence. It is a nerve-wracking attitude towards the end!

"See here, Madame, can you not once and for all tell me what your problem is?"

"You don't know?"

I am in a stew over this interrogation. Perhaps if I had the horo-scope of this client before me, would I see the matter more clearly? But how can I make her understand that I am not a diviner? Never-theless, I review in my mind the two terms of the charade; and I look angrily for the link that ties them: not married and not free! An instant more of groping, then the solution appears. Yes, the bearing, the allure of my client, confirm my intuition!

"Well, Madame, I have only made a hypothesis . . . ; but I am scarcely accustomed to it, I assure you."

"You see, sir, that the case was not so commonplace!"

"Yes, Madame, that is certainly the case! 'He', is a priest?"

By way of response, my client's gaze plunged towards the floor!

And little by little, in monosyllables, she told me how she had been smitten by her father-confessor, a man of liberal ideas and one indulgent of human weaknesses, and of commanding appear-ance to boot; how, step by step, she had made him discover the sentiment that she felt for him.

I asked again:

"And 'he', Madame, what does he say about it?"

The priest in question seemed to have lent a complaisant ear to these exalted confessions up to then, but it was perhaps in order not to be brusque with one of his flock. He seemed from that mo-ment on to have become stiff in his attitude, and that drove his adoring one to despair. Despairing of her cause, she had come to ask me whether her culpable amours had any chance of coming to a desirable end!

It was very painful for me to be useful to this client, who had despised morality, and who had only desired one thing—that she be told that the stars were favorable to her.

In fact, perhaps she was even expecting that I would propose to her to cast a spell on her confessor, to prepare a love potion for him, and to bring him to her feet, overwhelmed by passion and ready for the ultimate surrender!

It is strange how certain women, when they are possessed by this sort of amorous fury, lose all power of reason! I knew another one of this sort, the wife of a very respectable civil servant, and mother of a family too, who, having been unable to find any nourishment of her own temperament in her marriage, became foolishly enamored, at the onset of the critical age, with a young fellow two times younger than herself. That client, at least, gave no evidence of any timidity, she even gave proof of a frankness which touched upon cynicism in her account of their amorous indecencies, taking delight even in the recollection of certain equivocal details. In short, hers was an entirely instinctive passion, bursting forth after having been previously restrained, and which flowed like a wave swollen by a flood. She wanted to leave her husband and her children to follow her lover; and she wanted to know if happiness was awaiting her in that venture.

It was useless to consult the stars to be convinced that that project was one of inconceivable frivolity and one that would lead her to her ruin. I did it nevertheless, to acquit my own conscience, while seasoning my verdict with judicious counsels and reasons as solemn as possible. She thanked me for "the good will that I displayed in trying to keep her on the right road," but she told me that her decision was made and that she had already promised her lover to accompany him in his flight. I learned, however, some years later, from her own mouth, that she had succeeded in safeguarding her home by a sudden burst of lucidity and a spirit of sacrifice that had invaded her at the very last moment. Her "partner" was a drug addict! I have quite often shuddered to think into what wasp's nest that unhappy woman would have blundered if she had lacked sufficient self-control in the face of temptation.

Less tragic is the case of that correspondent who one day sent me his birth data, and that of seven or eight young women of his acquaintance. He asked me to make comparisons of his horoscope with those of his "favorites," in order to determine the one among them whose character and destiny would best harmonize with his own. Evidently a perfect idea of a very practical nature; one could only regret one thing—that the young man in question had not already been able by himself to reduce the number of "possible fiancées." I hope at least that the pertinent considerations that were sent to him were able to draw him away from his indecision!

If this kind of consultation evidently offers nothing commonplace, and if it partakes even of an elevated genre, how many times on the other hand does one fall upon entreaties that are absolutely exasperating!

The young woman who confuses astrology with clairvoyance is one of a legion; and it is with the best faith in the world that she asks you to give her a complete physical portrait of her future spouse, and you must not forget to specify the color of his hair and the expression of his eyes. Evidently, one can always strive to satisfy her, but experience shows that the more one searches for detail in astrology, the greater the risk of error becomes.

Besides, how many women consult the stars in the secret hope of seeing their projects confirmed—projects now and then born of a singularly exalted imagination!

One of them, breaking the quarantine, and having had dreams of fortune, wanted to know a day whose conditions would be the best for her: an administrative job, business, or . . . marriage. Marriage being very little promised by her natal chart, I counseled her strongly to enter some business dealing in deluxe items or in millinery, for which her chart showed that she was very well equipped.

But this counsel did not have the gift of pleasing her, for she had set her head on marrying a certain high functionary with whom she had already engaged in some friendly relations. She also especially wanted me to catch a glimpse of the desired union before long.

I strained my conscience as far as casting the horoscope of this eventual husband. And, as the comparison of the two charts did not promise any good aside from a simple exchange of fantasies, I said to her, by way of confirming my counsel to her, that she should turn herself by preference to business, to prospects more certain and more lucrative.

This turned out badly for me, for that client, very disappointed by my conclusions, disparaged astrology for its inability to predict the things desired, and which consequently **must** inevitably come to pass!

Along the same line, how many times has a client, on receiving a study in which the outlines of his future were announced to be very shocking, sent the work back to me, saying that I was deceived, that such eventualities **could certainly not happen** to him! Time, unfortunately, took it upon itself eventually to open his eyes!

Moreover, I could have gained many fortunes if I had been willing to play the game of certain clients, who, believing me to be an occultist, offered me much money for either a lucky piece or a love charm. Or who, even more unconscionable, asked me to cast an evil spell on a rival or to win for them the favor and the fidelity of a man with whom they were smitten. In many cases, a simple pretence of a casting a spell would have sufficed to open wide the purse of these "clients"; for I realized that they were entirely possessed by their passion and ready to do anything to satisfy it.

In such cases, I have made these lost sheep of love to understand in a friendly manner that they were deceiving themselves in their pursuit. And in the case where some cure did not seem impossible, I used to follow this declaration up with an attempted moralization that was very indulgent; but the result obviously varied according to the case.

This calls to mind the method—which was quite the opposite—of a self-styled fakir with whom I became acquainted one day, and who truly did possess some powers of black magic. He came moreover to pretend to entrust me (despite the distrust he had aroused) with certain books and instruments that he was eager to go to resell to his profit. But he, at least, didn't deceive his clients; for an agreed price of five hundred to a thousand francs[40]—according to their apparent intentions—he promised to cast whatever kind of spell of hate or love that was requested. His office, furnished with impressive objects—skulls, a stuffed owl, toads pierced by pins, waxen effigies, etc.—all bathed in a dim light that made to stand out even better the physiognomy, at once ironic and enigmatic, of the master within. Behind him, on the chimney, stood some glass jars in a row, apparently empty, but carefully stoppered. When anyone looked like he was going to approach those globes or lean over them, in order to discern their content, the fakir in question, with a startled air, very cleverly feigned, would rush in exclaiming:

"Don't touch them, you wretch! Those jars are full of elementals!"

From then on, the client could no longer have any doubt that the speaker truly had at his disposal legions of good and evil spirits, and his "magnanimity" was simultaneously facilitated and increased.

Truly, the profession of astrologer does sometimes have its picturesque aspects; but what is annoying is that this picturesque aspect is often confounded with ambiguity!

It is a more elevated concern, and one very estimable in princi-

---

[40] Translator's Note. Roughly $250 to $500 in today's money.

ple, that drives some correspondents to ask me to calculate for them the most propitious moment for the conception of a perfect child! Some would be satisfied—and much more reasonably so—merely to have an heir (or an heiress) as well off as possible.

It is in such demands, I believe, that resides the most unreasonable pretence that an intelligent man can nourish! If, in fact, it is perfectly possible to choose a chart that is ideal for a conception or a birth, how can one act so that that conception or that birth will take place at the desired moment? If one would recollect that fecundation can follow the moment of union by a whole day or even more, one must then take account at that point of the fact that the most careful calculation is revealed to be a wasted effort when faced with this physiological incertitude. In these circumstances, to determine a day favorable for conception is about the most that one can reasonably pretend to be able to do. And even if the child has been born or has been conceived on the chosen **day**, that is to say under fortunate configurations, thus avoiding for him any great dangers and painful difficulties, that same **moment** of birth could orient his horoscope in such a manner that his rising (or oriental) sign might be the worst one of all on that day. And thus again he would not necessarily gain a rosy existence, the sign of birth being unavoidably discordant with regard to the rest of his horoscope, and greatly attenuating its good presages.And since, in practice, the very best natal chart is never exempt from doubtful or malefic influences, one understands that those, by the chance of the hour of birth and the resulting distribution of the planets in the twelve houses of the chart, can very well supersede the better influences. Furthermore, one sees that destiny continues to defy the man who would have believed that he had locked it up in the nets of his dialectic; and the most learned calculations will never prevail against this truth!

I also became acquainted with a naive type of client, one who, having preserved himself as a virgin up to age forty—at least, he pretended to have done so!—wanted me to tell him from his fiancée's horoscope if it had given proof of the same reserve as his.

That time, I almost burst out laughing!

In the course of my career a number of sticky questions have evidently been put to me; the ones to which I shall make allusion will permit me to place in evidence the side of prognostic astrology that is somewhat "cynical."

One day a correspondent asked me, by way of curiosity and verification, to set forth for him the "revelations" of his chart for the previous ten years. In general, he was struck by the exactitude of certain forecasts; however, he remarked to me that I had not breathed a word about his marriage, which had occurred unexpectedly during the course of the period studied, and whose date he gave me.

I had to do my calculations over again, and I found nothing of the sort for the indicated date; but, among the forecasts that I had formulated, there appeared two years earlier, one of the "possibility of a union likely to come to a bad end."

The client finally had to confess that this was indeed the year in which he had "known"—in the biblical sense—his wife, who had died some years later. Thus, the prediction suddenly took on all its meaning.

Another time, a lady consulted me on the subject of what chances might exist of an understanding between two young people who had just become engaged. Having finished my careful examination, I concluded that there would rapidly be a misunderstanding and a probable separation if they married. The lady then confessed to me that the young people in question had in fact just broken off their engagement, and that she had only wanted to know from an interpreter of astrology if this separation was written in the stars.

How many times have I seen a marriage made at a moment when I had only forecast a profitable association! In fact, it is almost always then a question of a simple marriage for business interests or a marriage of convenience, in which sentiment plays no role. It is scarcely astonishing then that the material side was found to be prime motive. Many times I had to endure the criticism of certain clients who reproached me for not having indicated the death of a near relative, although an important material advantage, probably by a gift, had been predicted for them at the time when a corresponding inheritance had effectively fallen due to them.

This criticism offended me, for it is rarely that an important death can be foreseen so exactly. In similar cases, I have limited myself to posing the question:

"Were you on terms of affection with the deceased?"

Almost always it was confessed that the death in question had not caused any regret, and that it had even appeared rather like a kind of relief. Another time, the horoscope revealed the fact under the real physiognomy and not under the deceiving mask of appearances and conventional hypocrisies.

I would not finish by citing some more or less analogous episodes, but they all recall certain types of cases. Besides, all of them lead us toward the conclusion that it is necessary to use astrology wisely, reasonably, in the manner that I have indicated, and not to try to draw forth from it, either for yourself or for others, a destiny that is "all roses without any thorns" that one is pleased to imagine—quite wrongly—as being the ideal destiny.

On the contrary, it is necessary to accept the struggles and difficulties of existence; it is even almost necessary to wish for them, for they alone forge character; and the only thing that we can usefully ask of astrology is for it to make known to us the date or the period when the problems that concern us will present themselves and the form under which they will appear.

Thus, let us not try to alter the course of events which must befall us, but let us try chiefly to modify our attitude towards these events. It is not so much on the events themselves, but rather on their consequences, that our free will can act. It does not depend on us, at least on our being supermen, to turn aside from our path an eventuality that is sinister or simply unpleasant. But the sole fact of accepting that ordeal with courage, of looking for ways to limit its effects, already neutralizes its most painful aspect. To attempt to suppress from one's destiny, by a too egotistical calculation, everything that is not attractive or advantageous to oneself, springs from an infantile attitude, which shows that one has understood nothing about the problem of life.

To speak occultly, that is a kind of black magic that often rebounds against those who make usage of it.

Some painful and sorrowful experiences are everyone's lot; what matters, and where the true meaning of our life resides, is the reaction—energetic or more or less lax—that we are going to demonstrate when we contact these experiences. For it is these reactions themselves that condition the meaning of our future experiences, a constructive spirit being for us the best assurance of better circumstances in the future. That is the entire secret of a happy destiny; and that is all the aid that astrology can bring to us.

The Speculation in Images

But the most picturesque incidents in which I have been involved concern the *Financial Bulletins*, of which I have already spoken, and which were closely associated with them.

I have stated how, having focused at my own expense on a sufficiently coherent theory of astral influences on things relating to the stock exchange, I was led to publish, beginning in 1930, some monthly and daily forecasts that rapidly obtained a certain favor. At that time, having still a rash faith, given by my first success, I was even going so far as to publish some advance diagrams showing the presumed fluctuations of the trend. Experience has since demonstrated to me that such diagrams can do more harm than good.

May I be permitted first to say some words about these forecasts; they will define the atmosphere sufficiently!

It was at the very at the beginning of the publication of these Bulletins—during the course of their first year of existence—that a remarkable success took place, called "the Hoover Boom," which sanctified the renown of this publication of a new sort, destined to cause a certain sensation.

Imagine the times then! The Stock Exchange, the Temple of realist and positive spirits, open to the reveries of dreamers! This is what the publication of the first of these Bulletins signified, or so it appeared. How it was gloated over! He was laughed at pretty hard, that presumptuous astrologer, who believed he could talk to the traders as if they were simple servants or naive young ladies. As for me, convinced that I was in the right, I let them talk!

Then came the month of June 1931! My diagram for that month, very nearly steady up to about the 20th, showed a very lively flight for the last ten days, then continued its curve until around the 10th of July, then fell back a little before the 15th as brutally as it had risen three months earlier.

Gradually, as the date of the 20th approached, I became more and more anxious! Something was wrong! Some audacious financiers, on the strength of some successful forecasts, had taken an interest in my Bulletins and subscribed to them. What were they going to think if bad luck would have it that this time events would go against me?

For, although I had thought a lot and searched, I could discover no reason for a move higher in the market!

It is true that if the reason for it had been perceptible, the market would already have reacted automatically, but in any case I have always recalled the conversation that I had on Saturday, the 19th of June with a local banker, as anxious as I was to note the success or failure of my forecasts.

"I would really like to know," he asked me, "on what grounds you based yourself to predict your high?"

I confessed that I myself had not seen any plausible explanation that favored my prediction, but that I had to trust blindly in my system, from which, because of the previously experienced results, I had drawn a sufficient confidence. I was only able then to produce the figures I had obtained without trying to explain them. My banker friend fell easily into agreement with it.

"All the same," he avowed to me, "I have not dared to take a position at the high; but nevertheless, just out of pure curiosity I would like to be eight days older!"

The afternoon of that same day, I ran through the newspapers eagerly hoping to find mentioned in them some event that would justify my market conclusions. Alas, I found nothing! Due to that, I passed a pretty bad night making some bitter reflections on the awful disillusionment and the vexations of all kinds that no doubt awaited me in the course of the following days.

Sunday morning, having arisen very nervous and later than my custom, I eluded my discouragement in a thousand ways and only took notice then of the newspapers towards the end of the morning. An enormous headline was stretched across the front page: "President Hoover grants a moratorium to Germany." I ran through the article feverishly; in fact, its sensational character made me suppose that it could very well have some relation to the rise foreseen in my diagram. But in spite of everything I maintained a serious doubt! It took an unexpected encounter with one of my friends' stock-broker to reassure me almost entirely.

—You have read the news?, he asked me.

—Yes! What do you think about it? Will it have an effect on the stock market?

—It is the rise, my friend! And I also have the feeling that it will not be an ordinary one!"

I could almost have jumped for joy! How impatiently I waited for the next day! Again, I hardly slept, but this time it was my optimistic excitement that was the cause of it!

Monday, after noon, I was waiting in the colonnade of the Stock Exchange for the first news of the session. From the opening, most of the prices showed a rise of around twenty percent. At the end of the session, a great majority of the stocks closed at thirty percent above their lows of the preceding week! At a stroke, my banker's skepticism was shed with a sort of astonished admiration.

This first important success obviously won me several days of celebrity. But my glory quickly declined! The Stock Exchange digests news rapidly. After a long period of stagnation, it in fact recovered all its fine confidence! The rise was certainly only beginning! From then on, why would anyone have paid any attention to what a loud-mouth who had just had an extraordinary stroke of luck might have to say? The course to follow was simple—it was only necessary to buy! That is what they were saying in the Stock Exchange! During that time, playing the sinister prophets, I was putting my subscribers on guard against all excessive enthusiasm, and I drew their attention to the date of the 13th of July. I asked myself with a certain uneasiness if I was going to be right a second time!

But once again astrology scored a point! On the news of the failure of the Kreditanstalt Bank of Vienna, on the 13th of July, the market fell back sharply to the prices prior to the Hoover Boom! The public was astonished!

But it was quite another thing when you understand that my subscribers alone, or almost alone, had sold in time. At a stroke, I became a sacred prophet, reputed to be infallible. Among the speculators, who are more superstitious than one can even imagine, I suddenly acquired the reputation of a demigod! I was overwhelmed with attention, flattered, discussed. A clever man would have known how to exploit this craze and in a few days would have laid the foundations of a fortune.

At the risk of passing for a simpleton, I confess that that idea never occurred to me. The glory of astrology interested me more than money. I continued to disseminate my advice to a clientele which had suddenly increased on all sides.

Alas! Glory clings to very few things! Gods who do not continually make miracles quickly lose their adorers! A speculator came to consult me a little before the Kreuger crash, in order to know whether in my opinion his position was sound. He had quite a large portfolio of stocks at the high! I expressed to him my fears as to the imminence of a retracement. However, here too, no apparent circumstance seemed to give me any reason! Also, I immediately saw that that man was entirely helpless. I understood that it was hard for him to make a decision!

Nevertheless, he seemed determined beforehand to put his trust in me, and he closed out his position. The crash of the Swedish banker,[41] occurring unexpectedly some days later, permitted him to realize a substantial profit. He returned to find me, not knowing how to express his gratitude to me, and again soliciting my advice. Drawing his inspiration from it, but very boldly doubling his position, he again assured himself of a gain accordingly! And then, totally astonished at this easy success, and despite my advertisements, he again doubled the figure of his operations. But then, realizing himself the risk that he was running, he only dared to take a position in options under some forcibly burdensome conditions. Alas! When the time came to close out his position, he found himself in a profit position, as foreseen, but in an amount insufficient to cover the amount of forfeit that he had to pay. At a stroke, my star paled; my client lost confidence, he sought a system that was still more certain, which had no room for any risk; I hope that he has found it.

And that is how, while being right, the inconsistency of a client is sometimes sufficient to give you the appearance of being wrong!

But all my subscribers were not of so simple a character!

One day I received a visit from a local stock-broker, who, having heard my successes spoken of, wanted to reassure himself personally of their reality and of the foundations on which they were based. I furnished him all the convincing technicalities and the appropriate details. Sunk in his armchair, he listened to me talk with an air of skepticism, of detachment, and of ironic superiority, which intrigued me and discouraged me all at the same time. Suddenly, he got up, brusquely stood in front of me, and, looking at me coldly in the eye, he asked in the tone of the gentleman whom one cannot deceive:

—All that is very well. But what kind of group is behind you?

---

[41] Translator's Note. Ivar Kreuger (1880-1932), the "match king." Facing financial ruin, he shot himself on March 12, 1932, and his financial empire collapsed causing great losses to many investors.

That skeptical trader reasoned like a trader, and he was unable to comprehend that anything could exist outside of schemes and the maneuvers of outside brokers. I had much difficulty in convincing him of his error. And he kept on asking for a long time whether I was not making fun of him.

I also made the acquaintance of the villainies of the financial press.

There exist certain small market journals that live entirely off of their publicity, a publicity that is often equivocal, bordering somewhat on blackmail. One of these papers had sounded me out with a view to a series of advertisements that would have presented and extolled my financial bulletins. Having a horror of publicity for affairs of this kind, I had declined the offer. It was then that the blackmail—blackmail set in motion in the classic form of scathing articles—entered the game!

One fine morning, a previously unknown person presented himself at my office before it was open for business. I received him all the same. He wanted to be informed about my bulletins and my financial forecasts, and he asked me a series of questions. I furnished him my customary references with adequate details. He left me with a satisfied air, promising to think it over.

Some days later, I was surprised to see appear in the paper whose offer I had declined, a rancorous article in which I was ridiculed and depicted as a charlatan who was taking advantage of the public's credulity. The author wondered why the justice system had not come down hard on people of my sort, when it was authorized to do so by certain articles of the penal code—those famous articles of another age aimed at fortune tellers, interpreters of dreams, and in general those who exploited the naiveté of the masses.

I replied in strong terms to this indelicate "moralist," who had thus abused my confidence and my good faith. The financial journal in question, which had imagined that after that lampoon I would without doubt come to repentance, printed my protest, but blamed the attempt to beat me down on the caprice of a journalist in want of copy. There is no doubt that the journal recognized that it was on the wrong track! But its shot had missed, and that was the essential thing for me.

And on the contrary, the measured tone of my protest and the arguments developed in it had the result of attracting some new adepts to me, a result that my mastersinger had certainly not foreseen!

The unreasonable demands of our subscribers with regard to the exactitude of my forecasts sometimes necessitated some serious "explanations."

I sometimes had to deal with a powerful opponent among certain ones of them, which was truly very difficult. The bulletins in question were not presented—I have already had occasion to say this many times—as a product of pure divination, but rather as a kind of assessment of probabilities, capable of being verified in the proportion of 85%. Nevertheless, certain clients thought that the highs or the lows should be forecast with an absolute precision on the exact day. That is entirely proper if they were not relying on what would fix for them the course that would attain such an action on such and such a particular date! I remember that in certain bulletins I had forecast a high in the market for the 17th of the month. Now, a low was dominating the market at that moment, and on the 16th the market was still crumbling; on the 17th there was a new reaction, rather slowly in fact, but that appeared to extend to the 18th. On that day I received a telephone call from a subscriber who abused me vigorously because my prediction had not taken place on the precise day. As he seemed to me to be overexcited and was refusing to listen to my explanations, I politely asked him to go find another system of investment guidance. Besides, he did not have to wait very long to convince himself that he could at the least have spared me his excessive reproaches; in fact, on the 19th the market turned around, and in the days that followed it recovered strongly!

Among the subscribers to the financial bulletins, I encountered some types who were eminently curious, but rendered sympathetic by their very cynicism! I cannot resist the desire to put two of them in this gallery of picturesque portraits.

It was some years before the present war at a time when the bulletins were perhaps at the peak of their popularity. Their maximum print-run, limited to 75 copies, had been raised for the moment to 100 copies; it was frequently spoken of—much too much indeed—at the Brussels Stock Exchange, where from this fact they gave the impression of being in many hands.

One afternoon, the visit of a stock-broker was announced to me. He had come with the intention of gathering documentary information. Nervous, categorical, not open to metaphysical subtleties, and 100% positive, he dominated the conversation from beginning to end. It was short and decisive; my visitor opened fire at the outset:

—I have been told that you are publishing some financial Bulletins and that you base your predictions on the stars, or something like that. Me, I don't understand it at all, and besides I don't believe in all your "whatchamacallits." But I want to say one thing, for some time now I have been losing everything that I have invested in the stock exchange! Yes, I work particularly with stock options. Now, almost all those who make up my opposition are continually taking me in, and I have noticed that they read your "stuff," that is, your bulletins. So, whether you base your predictions on the stars or on whatever it is, I have come to ask you to show me one of your papers.

I showed him an example of the most recent monthly Bulletin.

—No, it is not that, he said to me. It is a different "whatchamacallit," in which you give the tendency for each day.

I then handed him a specimen of the weekly bulletin; I saw his face light up—

—Yes, That's it! That is what I have seen in their hands. From now on, guys, you won't get me any more! And how much does it cost, a subscription to that "stuff" there?

I indicated to him the price of a subscription. He immediately left me a wad of banknotes. He would have paid full price for the subscription if it had been double or triple what I had asked!

Then he went away satisfied, muttering again that he did not believe in all those "tricks," and that he didn't understand a thing about it, but that he certainly had to fight with weapons equal to those of his adversaries.

One time only, I was not able to restrain myself from making some singular reflections. So then, in spite of the desired limit on the number of subscriptions, and although there had only been thirty or thirty-five subscribers at the maximum in Brussels itself, it happened that some of them met each other all the same. How would it have been if the number of subscriptions had not been limited and there had been no restrictive conditions, if thousands of traders had been in possession of the same "secrets"? What a fine ferment? What a fine moral swindling? This had been, all the more rare, an affair analogous to the Hanau Affair, of picturesque memory. When I would say to you that it was easy to build a fortune on astrology! To make the public believe that it possesses a confidential source of information, and, on the contrary, to distribute that information in thousands of copies—that was, one will admit, a famous formula that guaranteed a fortune!

But on the contrary, my principal concern was always to limit the beneficiaries of the bulletins to a very small number; the total generally ran between fifty and seventy-five. Once in a while, as I was saying above, the figure rose to a hundred.

Still, some references were asked for before accepting a subscription! Not exactly moral references, but references of a commercial sort, establishing the fact that the subscriber was sufficiently familiar with market transactions and possessed a sufficient financial situation. What purpose would it have served to enter as a subscriber a small speculator with an insignificant capital, a capital that at the least error would have been swallowed up! That would have been the danger for me and the danger for you! And at the least a great moral responsibility!

These scruples—that some would have judged to be exaggerated—very probably saved me too from certain vexations.

In fact, the financial section of the Brussels Exchange had wind at one time of the existence of our financial Bulletins. Was it acting on its own account or on the indication of some "charitable soul"? I have never known. But nevertheless I was invited to furnish the Exchange all the useful references relating to my stock market activities. Doubtless, someone did suspect a form of exploitation of the public credulity. Because of this I had to submit to a stringent investigation; but, in spite of the skepticism that my statements encountered at the beginning, I finally succeeded in establishing that I had acted perfectly correctly in this matter. To shore up my statement, I even exhibited some letters in which I had been asked to publish certain ambiguous advertisements in *Demain*, but I had flatly declined these offers in spite of the loss of revenue that I would have realized. In short, I left that interrogation cleansed of all suspicions and congratulated to boot.

A second anecdote will illustrate the mentality peculiar to the milieu of stock traders!

I have said that, although our bulletins were printed in a very small number of copies, they made quite a bit of noise in the Brussels stock market. This fact was probably due to certain subscribers, who, lacking in discretion and very careless of their own interests, were communicating the tenor of our bulletins to some of their confreres. I even discovered one who was reselling complete and textual copies of our monthly Bulletins for his own profit! On the other hand, by my having published the essentials of my system in my book, *Fluctuations boursières et influences cosmiques* [Stock market Fluctuations and Cosmic Influences], I had inevitably formed some pupils, indeed some emulators.[42]

---

[42] I learned somewhat later that it had been precisely on the complaint of one of

Among our subscribers there was a stock broker who had a clientele of large banking establishments, and who was what is called an "animator"[43] of the market. His actions and activities, and especially his interventions were always observed, indeed spied upon, as a barometer of the trend.

On several occasions, that subscriber had assured me with the greatest seriousness that our Bulletins were too wide-spread in the Exchange, that they were the ones that were making the trend—in short, that I was a sort of *Deus ex machina* on the Brussels market. That assertion had always foolishly amused me, so much so that I was always asking myself if my client was speaking seriously.

However, he always made use of the same language! It was an obsession! One morning, when he had just received the latest monthly Bulletin, in which I had announced the imminence of a big high, he called me on the telephone, and, to my great astonishment, used the following language, which was, I must avow, entirely different from that which he had used previously:

—I have just, he said, received your bulletin in which you are announcing a high. I do not know whether you have taken a position based on that; but, if you have, I strongly recommend that you close it. You are going to have—I am saying this to you!—a big low instead of the predicted high!

And as, a little disconcerted, I did not reply, asking myself on what this rather unusual declaration was based, he continued:

—Yes, I have already had the occasion to tell you that you have become something of an encumbrance to us with your Bulletins! One might believe that we no longer existed, that we could not do anything! Well! We are going to show you that we can still do something; we are going to drive down the market prices. You're going to see a fine piece of work! Hang on good, and warn your subscribers if there is still time!

---

them, who had had certain brushes with the law, that I myself had been the subject of an inquest in the circumstances reported above.

[43] Translator's Note. What we would call a "market maker" or "market driver."

During this little discourse, I had had time to recover my spirits and to recall the configuration that had motivated my prognostication of a high. All the same, I was a little troubled by his categorical statements; but, confident of my own experience, I simply replied:

—Sir, I thank you for being so obliging. But in my turn, let me give you some good advice! You can certainly drive down the market prices if you want to, at least if you have sufficiently powerful means to do so. But in that case, do it promptly; for, in my opinion you will not be able to sustain that maneuver for very long, and the general trend will rapidly submerge it.

—We shall certainly see, he replied to me. In any case, you have been warned!

Effectively, with the support of a group that was important at that location, that "animator" succeeded in lowering the market prices by about five percent in the space of two days. That was the beginning of a panic! One after another my subscribers telephoned me asking me if there was not some error on my part.

I explained to them what I had learned, inviting them to become buyers at the bottom of the market prices and to be patient a little longer.

Actually, two days later, the market rebounded and did so with a vigor even greater than that with which it had been artificially repressed. I was assured later that my client had been stripped of his feathers in that affair! That would not have been unlikely!

It can be seen from some of these facts that I have just reported how delicate the management of financial prognostication is, and what interests and what states of spirit it sometimes runs afoul of. Several times too, I may say that I was on the point of radically suppressing the financial Bulletins. But, practically speaking, the system of subscription that was in effect, constituted a sort of interlocking mechanism whose functioning it would be very difficult to stop. Besides, the subscribers themselves would be the first to protest, and for every one who would declare himself indifferent to the suppression, there would be twenty or twenty-five who would express their desire to see our financial publications continue their career.

I believe that the formula itself of these subscriptions was simple and honest; but, in proportion to the benefits that it permitted the subscribers to realize or the losses that it enabled them to avoid, it was not sufficiently remunerative; for the preparation of the prognostication involved the true work of a dedicated student. For my part, I was satisfied all the same, my essential goal being to convince and to balance the budget of my Society.

Life is thus marked by experiences, some of them happier than others. In a path for which no guide exists, for which it is necessary to improvise everything, I have the impression that I have not managed too badly and of having arrived at my goal without major damage.

Can One Speak of an Astrological "Science"?

Coming immediately after the preceding chapter, in which I deplore in passing the excesses or the errors of certain astrologers, that question already loses its pertinence in the eyes of those readers who are inclined to judge things on appearances. For that reader, a science that leads to sometimes inexact conclusions is not a science! But that is too quick a judgment!

Along this line, it would be sufficient for me to put in evidence some famous surgical errors or some current therapeutic failures, in order to condemn medicine. Some discordances in the prediction of the weather by the observatories would also permit me to pretend that the art of meteorology is a fantasy. And I could extend the same systematic denigration to a good many other sciences besides those.

Would this be a valuable criticism? Assuredly not! To judge a science sanely and objectively, it is necessary first of all to ask whether it is an exact science or not.

Mathematics is an exact science; geometry can pass for that too; astronomy is almost an exact science. Medicine and meteorology are diagnostic sciences—in a word, empirical sciences, based upon experience, upon the repetition of certain things in analogous conditions; these are not exact sciences, but simply sciences of probability. Likewise, astrology is a science of probability; it is absolutely incapable of predicting **with certainty** what is going to happen, and I have shown previously the error of those who turn to it in the hope of seeing it put an end to their vexations. It can only recognize the field of destiny, mark out the routes that traverse it, reveal the dangers, track down the ambushes, and thus constitute a sort of tutelary guide.

When it is a question of determining the probable destiny of a human being, astrology must necessarily proceed as follows. First, establish the main lines of character and temperament in such a way as to take into account whether the reactions are instinctive or calculated; in the first case, it is a matter of a type that is essentially determined, and one will be able to predict very nearly on the mark that he will not avoid any of the dangers announced by his horoscope; in the second case, free will is already developed, and reflection will permit him to avoid a number of ambushes or to reduce their severity. Next, it is necessary to calculate the times when certain events are likely to occur, and the particular nature of these events,. Finally, and only then, is it possible to interpret these probabilities in the light of what one has judged of the subject's nature itself.

One sees then the important part that diagnosis plays—that is to say, the **subjective** element—in the interpretation of an astrological chart. And this explains the fact that, no more than physicians, astrologers do not always agree among themselves. Worse still! that they are sometimes even of diametrically opposed opinions.

In such a case, it is not necessarily astrology that is at fault, but more likely the astrologer. But again, if one would bear in mind that the astrologer is only a human being, therefore imperfect and fallible, one would be inclined to understand and to pardon him.

But when the practitioner must judge abstract or collective facts, as is the case in mundane astrology, for example the signing of treaties, International Conventions, or declarations of war, the diagnostic difficulty increases immeasurably. For the investigator does not have at his disposal the indices that permit him to estab-

160

lish in what sort of spirit these kinds of events were crystallized, and, consequently, what the probability is that the facts proceeding from the state of the heavens at that moment may be realized along their natural lines or may deviate from them more or less. That would be possible only by establishing the horoscopes of all those personages who participate in the launching of these events; and what then! For one would thus wind up with a study that would be complex, confused, perhaps inextricable; but in any case, a veritable Chinese puzzle. Besides, since political personages succeed themselves rather rapidly on the world scene, it is easy to see what patience and what methods would be required to keep the astrological file up-to-date. One human lifetime would not be sufficient!

This is why, being necessarily obliged to cut it short, the astrologer judges and decides in this matter according to the demands of his own temperament. Generally, starting out from the principle that the mass of people act according to their instincts, he will decide along the lines of fatal necessity. But certain astrologers, listening to their passions, or taking their own desires to be realities, or again attributing to certain personages a wisdom that they do not possess, have a tendency to depart from those narrow limits that their calculations have locked their reason into. And from that errors arise that are sometimes astonishing, but which reveal themselves to be only human if one studies the process that has caused them.

Perhaps one would discern fewer errors in our science if the rules and the principles of astrological judgment were found to be established in a solid framework from which no essential element was lacking. Then, the most experienced astrologer would know how to handle any case no matter how unforeseen. Unhappily, we are still a long way from that; for astro-dynamics has not yet put together all the receipts that those possessed who were its Masters in the old days; and the tradition on which it leans is certainly incomplete or deformed.

Some statisticians have tried through observation to recoup the principles on which that tradition was mute or uncertain. Thus they hoped to rebuild by modern methods the framework to which I have just alluded. Unhappily, the laws of astral influence appear to be so complex, so complicated, that observation is more often powerless to disentangle the exact rules of the game, and that only the major laws, putting in play some very simple elements, let themselves be revealed.

So it is that if one had been able to establish, for example, the value of certain laws of heredity, or of ascendants in "air signs," or of certain aspects that govern certain abilities, one has still not been able to determine by statistics what are the exact differences of longitude that constitute what we call "aspects," nor what is the proper way to calculate the "Houses," nor what method of directions reveals itself to be the most efficacious. Now, there are three essential problems of astrology which have not been resolved! And, so long as they remain without a definite solution, astrology will necessarily "flounder" and will only give approximate results.

It is here that one can "put his finger on" how much a well established confraternity of astrologers could play a capital role in the advancement of their science. More understanding, more mutual contacts, would permit confrontations of theories and research that would singularly accelerate the attainment of the looked for results. There may be some laborious trials based on erroneous principles, the inutility of which would thus be demonstrated from the outset! How many others, by contrast, would find themselves very much more often supported and made precise by parallel efforts! And how astrological progress would stride like a giant!

Once more, one takes the opportunity here to deplore the fact that the astrological movement is not organized, disciplined, and governed by a competent Commission, which would safeguard the honor of the profession, distance itself from the scabby sheep, pass through a sieve the works of its members, communicate to everyone what seemed worthy of being retained, and thus create a profession, licensed in some fashion.

162

Alas! These are beautiful dreams that one can in good faith have believed to be realizable. But I have said elsewhere how much their attainment seemed to me to have become remote after one had seen in 1937 at the Paris Convention nationalism again steal a march on scientific cooperation.

As if science had any fatherland! As if science, the same as music, was not a universal language that can bring together men and peoples! I have never had either hatred or scorn for anyone; but I cannot comprehend how one can commit the sacrilege of slighting this language and attacking its sublimity.

Happily, in the meantime, astrology makes up for the lack of official instruction by its own every-day experience and also by the exercise of an intuition that shapes and develops itself through contact with realities.

In this regard, it is undeniable that certain astrologers "feel" better than others the physiognomy that can take the play of influences written in the horoscope. Certain others, by contrast, excel in the exercise of logic, and, returning without exception to very simple principles, succeed in expressing the subtle differences to an infinite degree in their interpretation, everything in it affirming a trusty solidity. And, what is remarkable, is that almost always they arrive, by private and very often divergent methods, at obtaining similar or concordant results. In order to explain this phenomenon, I would be inclined to believe that their intuition has finished by adapting itself closely to the special run of their experiences, has finished by joining with it, and that, basing itself on the particulars quite proper to that experience that it alone has the power to observe, it recovers thus in passing the different landmarks that mark the same route.

I have seen some well-known astrologers apply themselves to the hard work of calculating primary directions and obtain only mediocre results. I have seen others who "tapping in the heap"—without one always being able to discern whether their conclusions were valid—limiting themselves to the simple observation of transits, or even just of conjunctions. Others, fierce partisans of symbolic directions—such as Eudes Picard and his students—drawing from them sometimes dazzling conclusions. And yet is there a system more rudimentary, in a word as little scientific, as that of symbolic directions?

It is evident that each system contains without doubt a part—but only a part!—of the truth, and that the knowledge of that part alone permits some results to be obtained, fragmentary without doubt, but which reveal themselves sufficiently in most cases.

For my part, while recognizing the theoretically superior technique of primary directions, I have not proven that in practice they were of an efficiency that was clearly better than the others. That is why I have maintained a preference for the system of secondary directions, whose scientific value is not to be disdained.[44] But as it allows, it too, some blank periods and some time-lags, I have completed it by a careful analysis of transits and of lunations; and I even ask myself if one day I will not limit myself to that analysis alone. It is, however, very difficult in these kinds of things to determine the system that marks the seconds—that is to say the instant of the launching of events—and the one that marks the hours—that is to say the approximate epoch when these events come to maturity. And by the fact of a simple coincidence, one can very easily believe that one possesses a good system, when some subsequent experiences permit us to take into account the part that chance has played in obtaining the results.

One of my clients, the proprietor of an important pastry shop, presented himself one day at my office, quite evidently prey to an extraordinary emotion, and insisted, in order to speak to me immediately, that I should for that reason interrupt my consultation. He was coming to announce to me the verification, **to the exact day**, of the danger of an explosion that I had advised him of a short time earlier, either by a mechanical engine, or something else, but that

---

[44] In effect, the fact that after 365 solar days or 366 sidereal days there then exists a shift of one calendar day permits one to justify the relation 1 day = 1 year.

could happen at his home. Some hours earlier in fact the oven of his pastry shop had blown up; the damages, happily, were only material. I was obviously flattered by this report, but I refrained from being vain about it, for chance was certainly involved to some degree, even if only a minimal amount. If it had been otherwise, then all my prognostications would have had to occur on the exact date; now, it was in general necessary to count on—and there was already there an appreciable result, one will agree—a more or less sizable approximation, on a certain amount of "play." Scientifically speaking, I could not, therefore, draw a general conclusion from this particular instance, thereby deciding to make a rule of so exceptional an occurrence. Thus, chance often comes in for a part of the success or the failure of a prognostication, and statistics themselves would be powerless to determine the importance of that part.

Also, that is one reason more to have some mistrust vis-a-vis those "amazing" theories, almost always put forth with a force of conviction that overawes one because these theories repose most often merely on an appearance of reasoning. One could not repeat often enough how much these theories should be confronted—the more stringently the better—with strict reality. And again it is important to keep a cool head in making that confrontation, for a number of these theories are quite seductive from a spiritual point of view.

The facts or the verifications that are invoked in their favor are as a general rule notoriously insufficient to constitute a demonstration in the scientific sense of the word.

I believe I am able here to deplore the lack of scientific sense in most astrologers. Certainly it is not necessary to expect that a theory be proven in order to draw some deductions from it; but in such a case, they must be presented with the reservations that are required. These reservations are of importance in an epoch in which the public, most often ignorant of what astrology is, is naturally led to take for certainties everything that is presented to it as such. Then when, sooner or later, the affirmations in question are revealed to be counterfeit or exaggerated, it is astrology itself that suffers the repercussions. And if the public, good child that it is, passes quickly enough over this kind of error—for it too is superficial, as we have already seen, superficial and essentially lacking in the critical spirit—it is not the same with serious people, especially the scientific ones, who only give their verdict based on positive data.

Perhaps even the latter go a little too far with that kind of idea; and I allow myself to reproach them in passing. I have naturally had on numerous occasions to set forth my arguments in favor of astrology in the presence of men of science and of the universities, and among those whom I would characterize as being the most stubbornly opposed to my arguments—for example, Prof. Piccard—I have been able to establish undeniably that their counter-arguments consist of extending further and further the limits of the discussion, in such a way that finally it leaves firm ground to lose itself in quagmires. Prof. Piccard, for example, would not discuss that there could exist twelve human "families" corresponding more or less to the twelve signs of the zodiac; but he attributed to the influence of the Sun only those divergences that are present among these twelve families and not to any planetary influences. He made the remark that the products of vegetation or of nature at a certain moment of the year could have an equal effect on the constitution of the body, and consequently on its character; and that in addition the special characteristics of these products in certain particular regions must necessarily lead to some physiological differences. But the discussion was cut short when I suggested that, precisely, the divisions of animal and vegetable species, and even of minerals, could well be conditioned by planetary influences exercising themselves within the limits of time and space. For want of our being able to dwell upon an absolute fact, the two of us were thus reduced to opposing each other's suppositions. A scientific discussion appears impossible under these conditions.

Statistics themselves—and God knows how much labor certain ones had cost their authors—did not find favor with Prof. Piccard.

It is necessary to say in acquittal of the savants that they are generally overburdened with work and obligations, and that to form for themselves a judgment worthy of the name, it would be necessary for them to sacrifice numerous hours in the examination of questions in which they no doubt have no personal interest. On sees, therefore, the difficulty involved in interesting men of science in astrology, men who could by the weight of their testimony rehabilitate it. It is not everyday nor even every century that a William Crookes is found to proclaim, in defiance of his personal interest and the opinion of his peers, that Truth goes singularly beyond the framework that the solemn academies believe they have constructed—the academies that forget the declaration of Prof. Charles Richet: "Woe to the savant who believes that the book of nature is closed and that there is nothing more new to make known to weak men!"

For, adds Prof. Richet, "It is necessary to be persuaded that today's science, as true as it is, is terribly incomplete . . . All that science of which we are so proud is only the knowledge of **appearances!**"

In this regard, the discovery of the atomic bomb would have had some unexpected repercussions, not only on the material plane, at Nagasaki or at Hiroshima, but also on the moral and intellectual plane! For it would have shown to the most skeptical that, under familiar appearances, some forces are lurking, the power or the amplitude of which no one suspects.

Who would dare to pretend thereafter that astrologers do not possess a considerably greater part of the truth than one would have been tempted to believe at first? Whoever wants to take the trouble to follow their works attentively will convince himself very quickly that their value is scientific, although irregular. And he will admit that this science is worth the trouble [it would require] to be thoroughly investigated.

For my part, I have always declared that those who enter upon the study of astro-dynamics, even with incredulity, would become first convinced, then "supporters" or enthusiasts.

When in fact the student discovers that such-and-such a being reacts exactly as the study of his astrological chart has permitted us to forecast, when he verifies that certain violent configurations bring about "trains" of accidents or disturbances, that the wind obeys the aspects of Mercury, and that the Stock Exchange itself is sensitive to the aspects and the positions of the planet Jupiter, he has suddenly gained the impression that it contains a parcel of that mysterious power that rules the destinies of the world, and that events obey it as they do the astral influences.

Already, the power of the marvelous operates when it is a matter of simple appearances, indeed of vulgar illusions; but what intellectual and moral intoxication does it not give when the results obtained demonstrate without any possible question that it rests upon certitudes!

Perhaps one day the objective proof—that is to say the scientific proof, repeatable on demand, within the reach of all—of astral influence will be found! While we are waiting, let us be content with the subjective proof, which is equally accessible to all men of good will.

And in this regard, may I be permitted to hope that the predictions published during the last twenty years in the periodical *Demain* have been able to contribute to forming the religion of those readers who are skeptics but men of good faith. It does in fact not seem to me to be normal that chance would have been able to play so great a role regularly in the success of the greater part of them that anyone could call it coincidence. Especially when, most of the time, the technical justifications were given in connection with each prognostication. If certain ones of them have seemed to be a little more indistinct, one must not forget that most often the configurations to be interpreted are themselves very entangled, very confused or very contradictory. If it has happened that I have erred openly, is it necessary to be astonished? In this matter we are all exposed to being human. In fact, if I may be permitted to recall that criticism is easy, but art is difficult, and that since my predictions were written and not verbal, I do not even have the means—debatable enough, besides, but which is readily used—to alter after the fact their tenor or their spirit, to bring them into better agreement with reality.

But it is of course necessary to admit, on the other hand, that it departs from the framework of pure coincidences, to have foreseen **to the exact moment** certain important events, among which I recall in particular: the tragic death of King Albert, the death of King George V, the nearly conformable destiny of Hitler and Mussolini, the successive blows of force of the Third Reich that permitted it to reoccupy the left bank of the Rhine and assure its rearmament, Italy's attack on Albania, Germany's attack on Poland, the inconsistency of the Franco-British declaration of war in 1939, which had to lead to the dissociation of that alliance, lead France to a separate peace, and lead England into its decline, even in case of victory; the sufficiently consistent evolution of events during the course of the last war—with the exception of those affecting Russia—and notably the disasters that marked the onset of hostilities in the Pacific, the Allied landing in North Africa, and the armistice with Italy. And, are these events not taking now—Alas!—the deceptive turn announced in my predictions for 1945 and 1946 that were published more than a year in advance?[45]

I do not cite these successes out of any concern for vainglory, I have passed the age of those vanities. But one is accustomed to say, "God himself needs the church-bells"; and, therefore, it can be useful to recall those results that are striking enough and no less regular to the attention of the stubborn and skeptical.

More and more, besides, the learned are approaching our conceptions; to convince oneself of this, it suffices to re-read what is being written about astrology by some savants, such as Dr. Alexis Carrell, Dr. Nordmann, Dr. Jung, Prof. d'Arsonaval, Prof.

---

[45] See the special number of the Revue *Domain,* "A Turning in the History of the World," the work *The Mystery of Astral Influences,* and the "Reports" of the conferences given by the present author on the years 1945 and 1946.

Boutaric, Camille Flammarion, the Abbé Moreaux, and many others.[46] It is sufficient to state that more and more practitioners subscribe to new methods that are still disapproved of by official science. The increasing utilization of radio-electric detection by members of the medical profession, for example, constitutes a decisive demonstration of this fact. And, if graphology has almost achieved its warrants for use at the present time, there is no reason why astrology should not attain the same results sooner or later.

I think in this regard that one of the most fertile lines of research that can lead to the demonstration of astral influence, and to the possession of the keys that unlock it, would be that of terrestrial magnetism. Remy Brück, that little-known savant, has left to us in his report some very precious attestations, the examination of which, it seems to me, is of a nature to make us find the way. I incline to believe that a similar examination could explain to us why neither primary directions, secondaries, or the others regularly give us satisfying results.

Therefore, let us remain confident, in spite of the defeats and uncertainties of the present moment. One day, in a world made wiser and more enlightened, the science that is dear to us will pour out its benefits widely under the control of public powers.

---

[46] See *The Mystery of Astral Influences* by the present author.

From the Invasion of Belgium to the Rebirth of the Periodical "Demain"

On May 10, 1940, something happened to me that was very surprising for an astrologer. For isn't it true that an astrologer owes it to himself to foresee everything!

Perhaps! But then only on the condition of really wanting to do so.

I was taking the cure at Spa[47] in the first days of the month, and I had found there, on some high ground, near a grove of fir trees, a very pleasant hotel where one could truly find an ideal repose. An amusing detail: when, on my first day there, I wanted to make a telephone call, the host expressed his regrets: because of the crisis that was raging in the hotel industry following the mobilization, he could only count, he explained to me, on being reconnected the next month; furthermore, out of consideration for the repose of those taking the cure, no radio had been installed! As for the rest, the comfort was perfect, and the table was excellent.

On the 9th of May, in mid-afternoon, I took the classic walk to Hoëgne. Unfortunately, I missed the train that would have, on my way back, saved me more than an hour's walk, and, in order to pre-

---

[47] Translator's Note. A town in the Belgian province of Liège, known for its medicinal springs.

pare myself for the long trip that I had yet to make, I went in to rest at an establishment near a railroad bridge that was guarded by some Belgian soldiers stationed in a small fort, the muzzle of their machinegun pointed at the valley.

"See those unlucky boys," said the hostess, "They are on duty for twenty-four, or sometimes even, for forty-eight hours, without even being permitted to come over here to get some refreshment. Don't you agree that that is ridiculous!"

I recall, as if it were yesterday, the reply that I made:

"How would you have it, Ma'am; it is harsh without doubt; and the service could envision a more humane rotation, I agree with you! But bear in mind that discipline is indispensable in the present circumstances and that our cousins to the East, if they decide to invade us, will certainly not forewarn us! We must be constantly on our guard, whatever it costs.!"

At that moment, I did not imagine that only a few hours later my response would pass, in the mind of my interlocutor, for a sort of prophetic advertisement.

In fact, no danger seemed to hover over the beautiful valley of the Hoëgne; everything was laughing, welcoming, the air was gentle, the horizons peaceful, and only some pickets of soldiers scattered through the woods recalled to the stroller that the region was on a state of alert.

When I had been advised not to go on vacation at Spa, in an exposed region, I had laughed at that fear. I was in fact an optimist; not that I believed war to be impossible, but I had confidence in my good star. Besides, who would have been able to imagine that things would have occurred in a manner so sudden, so rapid, so disconcerting? Everyone, under the impression of "bluffing," who pretended that our army was well prepared and the Albert canal uncrossable, imagined that in case of an invasion the German forces would be stopped very near our frontiers. I would, therefore, have plenty of time to get back to Brussels after the first alert.

I returned to the hotel quite late, worn out by my long walk. I ate a good dinner, then I went to bed. But, due to my digestion and fatigue, I could not go to sleep. Also, I was surprised to notice some noises that I had not noticed during the course of the preceding nights; at some very short intervals, motorbikes and autos passed like a whirlwind under my windows. From that I concluded that I must have enjoyed some singularly restorative nights! Sleep finally came, but it abandoned me at dawn: mooing of cows in the meadows, droning sounds of airplanes, muffled detonations, the sky was furrowed with white trails.

—Another German "error"! I said to myself. What do those people want with us now?

And I went back sound asleep! But, with the suspicious rumors persisting, a silent uneasiness made up of a thousand abnormal details crowding the atmosphere in spite of everything, and the detonations continued, even growing nearer, I eventually got up at the stroke of nine, I went down to the dining room, still deserted. I was busy eating when a car stopped in front of the hotel, all one family—seven or eight people—and they got out with incessant exclamations. They asked for rooms. I faintly heard them say that they had received an order to evacuate Verviers,[48] and that they had come here to find a refuge.

—Well, good! Some more cowards, I said to myself rather thoughtlessly. and I began to watch the group.

It was thus that I learned with astonishment a half hour later that Germany had simultaneously invaded Belgium, Holland, and the Grand Duchy of Luxembourg; that Brussels had been bombarded; and that the German troops were on the outskirts of Hockai, three miles from us.

My immediate reflex was to jump into my car, drive into Spa, and assure myself there that there was really a state of war, but that flight was still possible.[49]

---

[48] Translator's Note. A town about 11 miles north of Spa.

[49] Translator's Note. Spa is about 70 miles east of Brussels as the crow flies, and

My concern, frankly, ended on an unforeseen circumstance! To pay my bill and get my bags ready was only an affair of a few moments. In short, around 10 o'clock in the morning, on that 10th of May 1940, I left Spa, persuaded that I was going to undergo some serious bombing, perhaps to run afoul of some patrols, and that the adventure would very likely end in the bottom of a ditch, in the hospital, or perhaps even in the beyond!

In fact, my return went just as it would have in a time of peace—which seemed to me abnormal and gave me an impression of uneasiness—and, in the early hours of the afternoon, without having seen a single French or English soldier, I re-entered Brussels, having seen by contrast the roads filled with refugees, and encumbered with the most diverse kinds of vehicles, the lamentable spectacle of bewildered families pushing before them in kiddie-cars or hand-carts everything that they owned. A grievous spectacle, and one that broke one's heart to be unable to offer any remedy!

I was inexpressibly happy about this unhoped-for return, I did not cease to thank my good star, and I awaited the course of events with confidence. The official communiqués were optimistic, they were being held on the Albert Canal.[50] However, I pricked up my ears when the radio reported some fighting at Tongres![51] Tongres? But then . . . was the Belgian defense then pierced? Would the propaganda always bluster then?

Then one saw flowing towards Brussels, not only the frightened civilians who were fleeing from the German terror, but some soldiers and up to some ranks who had come back to the capital as one stage of their flight and were getting ready to flee still further. They described with terror in their eyes the irresistible attacks of the German Stukas,[52] the incessant harassing on the roads, and the

---

perhaps 80 miles by highway—less than two hours drive normally.

[50] Translator's Note. A canal running NW from Liège to Antwerp. At Liege it is some 50 miles east of Brussels.

[51] Translator's Note. A town 12 miles NW of Liège.

[52] Translator's Note. Dive-bombers.

general disorder. This was the beginning of one of the most lamentable exoduses in history! By whatever means available, the frightened population sought their safety towards the south. More and more numerous, more and more packed together on the roads, they blocked all military traffic, vehicles of all kinds left the center of Belgium with a mattress fastened on the roof by way of protection—quite illusory—against airplane bullets. Some members of the public administrations, some functionaries ordered into service, deserted their posts thus, seized by panic. During the course of three days I could ask myself if the world had gone mad, or if I myself was stricken by lack of understanding. And during those three days I was asking myself whether I myself was going to let myself gain in some way from the surrounding fever! I finally decided not to leave Brussels, judging that contact with the German armies could scarcely be more dangerous than it had been in 1914-1918.

And it was thus that I saw enter into the capital—which had at one moment been on the point of being bombed—some German soldiers all sugar and honey. This then was the Belgian capitulation, the discourse of Reynaud that heaped shame on our heads, the break-through at Arras that the communiqués drew with mathematical exactness on the map,—and which some of my friends obstinately refused to believe, since that seemed so unlikely—the rush toward Paris and the abandonment of the capital, the French debacle, and to cap it all, the capitulation of our southern neighbors.

It was a disaster, a disaster that was not along the line of the astrological forecasts, which were on the contrary announcing the impossibility of a final success for the axis Powers. At one moment even I asked myself if the period of disorder that I had believed I saw for Germany in the following month of August was not on the contrary going to be one of unprecedented triumphs for them, and if the astrological forecasts were not going to be totally reversed. It is in fact known that in a conference given in 1939 I had announced a critical period for Germany in April 1940, the probability of a separate peace for France, and a formidable crisis for the British Empire, even in case of victory. Was that then going to collapse like a house of cards? But then, from whence would come something to neutralize this German success?

But the time passed, however, and the attack against the British Isles was never made. After that, the possibility of some sort of compromise peace became possible; but, so that such a peace would not be to our disadvantage, my astrological colleagues indicated that it would be necessary to wait until 1945, and perhaps even until 1946. That seemed incredible to me! And besides... that same lapse of time—as improbable as it was in 1940—had it not been required to triumph over Germany at the time of the First World War? It was, then, necessary to adapt oneself to the situation, and besides, all the governmental authorities enlisted the population to put themselves to work.[53]

A piquant detail: on all the streetcars then one saw as many people intent upon German behavior as one afterwards saw studying English behavior at the moment of liberation!

At the Revue *Demain*, the May number, ready for the press, obviously did not appear, and for a good reason! For us, the German occupation appeared as a catastrophe, for we probable would no longer be able to publish, and we were cut off from a good part of our foreign clientele, while the exodus must have scattered our Belgian and French readers somewhat.

The German administration, threatening with definite prohibition those newspapers and periodicals that did not submit a request for publication authority, we decided, with the unanimous consent of the active administrators, to submit our request, with the understanding that it would not be pursued if the conditions to which they would eventually agree were not agreeable to us. However, since *Demain* had never been involved in politics, and since it was

---

[53] In a financial bulletin that appeared on the 19th of August 1941, I assessed the chances of an Axis victory versus an Allied victory as follows: in 1941, 9 to 1; in 1942, 7 to 3; in 1943, 5 to 5; in 1944, 3 to 7; and in 1945, 1 to 9.

entirely a technical periodical, we could not see how our publication could have resembled any kind of collaboration. Some newspaper friends, consulted on this matter, were of the same opinion.[54]

However, we did not have long to debate our hesitations and our quite natural scruples. A letter from the Occupation brought to our notice that the periodical *Demain*, being without any public interest could not reappear. The matter had already been settled for us!

It only remained then for us to take the necessary measures to liquidate our Society. But, while Mr. Brihay said that he was in favor of ceasing our activities altogether and doing away with our archives, the Viscount de Herbais and myself were of the opinion that we should only "damp down" our activities to a degree that the Occupation would not prohibit them; [that way] we could remain in contact with those sympathetic to our movement, and—who knows?—still be of some use to them.

It was thus that our Society emigrated one day from the ideally situated offices that it was occupying in Sumatra Avenue to Uccle, in order to install itself at a reduced rate in a little mezzanine office on Midi Avenue where I had my own business.

And that lasted until the spring of 1941; a part of our clientele had returned to us, and our Society did as well as could be expected, each person accepting his own part of the necessary sacrifices. It was then that the unexpected event happened that led to the reappearance of our periodical.

One afternoon at the office I received a telephone call from Mr. Léon Wyckmans, our printer, in which there was a certain uneasiness, and by which he informed me that two Germans who wanted to speak to me had just called on him believing that they were at the [office of the] Revue *Demain*, and that he had given them my address.

---

[54] A racy detail: it was Mr. Brihay, who was then the manager of the Éditions de la Revue Demain, who personally drafted that request in German. At that time, the divergences of view and interest were yet to come forth.

And in fact, a few moments later, two Germans in civilian clothes entered my office; and the resultant conversation took place in French in the presence of my secretary, and through the interpreter of one of the two visitors, an under official of the German Embassy, who was serving as interpreter. the second of my interlocutors was himself an official of the Ministry of Foreign Affairs, who introduced himself—as amiably as a German could—on behalf of our former Swiss colleague Mr. K. E. Krafft.

I caught my breath. For a moment I had feared something else! The Gestapo perhaps!

—"Mr. Krafft," said Dr. . . . (whose name I cannot recall) "has spoken to me about your periodical and expressed his regret that it was no longer appearing. Why have you stopped publishing it?"

—Why? Simply because the German administration forbids us to publish!

—The German administration? Why? Had you published anything hateful against Germany before the war?

—Hateful, certainly not! We have never expressed any manifestation of any kind of hate. But it is possible that we may have published certain predictions which might have been judged to be displeasing by your services; please note in addition that in all instances we have written what we thought, without bothering to please or to displease anyone whatsoever.

—Mr. Krafft had the impression that, before the war, you had given evidence of being a strong Francophile.

—I do not see on what grounds Mr. Krafft bases a thought of that sort; but do not forget that we are a periodical of French expression. Mr. Krafft's opinion is somewhat amusing, for in the eyes of some Frenchmen we are considered to be Germanophiles.

—Germanophiles?

—Yes, and that is also false! But, since we were present at an international Convention at Düsseldorf, in which your Chancellor sent us a telegram of welcome, astrology is considered to have become a fascist science.

—The question for us, if I judge it according to the directives that have been given to the appropriate services, is not to know whether you have written anything disagreeable in our regard, but rather whether you have been shown to be a political or cultural enemy of Germany.

—We do not engage in politics, but only in science. And, I repeat, we give our conclusion entirely objectively, without any intent to flatter anyone whatsoever.

—Can you show me some numbers of your periodical in which you consider that you have published some things disagreeable to Germany?

—Certainly!

I submitted to my interlocutor, among others, a horoscope of Hitler, that appeared in our columns, when it was a question of an apogee for him around 1939, as well as some predictions that appeared before the invasion of Poland, in which the Axis intention of conquest was denounced and depicted as liable to a final failure. The Dr... made a wry face, but showed himself to be a good player.

—Can you show me some more numbers of your publication? he asked me.

He leafed through these numbers carefully, his face lightening or darkening according to whether what he was reading was favorable or unfavorable to Germany.

Finally, he handed me some issues of which he had taken notice, saying to me:

—Undoubtedly, I think that it would be wrong to view you as either a Germanophile or a Francophile! You seem to me to be sincere and objective. In view of this, I do not see why your publication should be prohibited.

—You see, however, that the German administration is not of

the same opinion as you!

—It may have judged superficially. Like every administration! But I am going to have your file reviewed, and there is no doubt in my mind that you will be able to resume publication of *Demain*.

—And yet can that be possible! We have practically liquidated our Society; our clientele is scattered. Conditions have changed a lot since 1939. And then, I would have to give up my present business. You can see that there are complications!

—But I believe that you would like to reappear?

—It was our intention in 1940; but, I repeat, circumstances have changed!

—But Mr. Krafft has spoken of a recent letter in which you are complaining of having to suspend your publication. And it is precisely to please Mr. Krafft that I have taken it upon myself to give you a visit in the hope of arranging things if that is possible.

—We have not made any request of that sort to Mr. Krafft![55]

(I understood later, in response to a letter of the latter asking him for news, that the Viscount de Herbais had declared without any afterthought "that everything was relatively good in the present circumstances, but that it was too bad that the Revue was banned, the Society being condemned on this head to almost complete inactivity")

Dr. . . looked at me, not understanding anything except that my sincerity was evident to him. He did not insist.

—However, he asked me, if you receive authorization for it,

---

[55] I may be permitted here to settle a point of history. The major press has made a lot of noise about K.E. Krafft. He has been denounced as having been Hitler's astrologer. Now, Mrs. Krafft and all his closest friends have always denied that; besides, the *Journal de Genève* seems to have refuted this accusation. Why, indeed, if that had been the case, would Krafft have been interned, and why would he have died unhappily at Büchenwald? And why did the British newspapers announce, when K. E. Krafft was already dead, the arrest of Professor Krafft, the Führer's astrologer? This mystery has still not been clarified, in spite of Mrs. Krafft's efforts.

will you start publishing?

—If it is at all possible, I would like to do it, but on the condition of having the same freedom of attitude that we had in the past.

—You are wanting to discuss censorship? Censorship does not pose any problem for a technical Revue such as yours.

—That already removes certain difficulties. But anyway, the decision is not mine alone. I must consult with my colleagues.

—Get their advice then! While waiting, I am going to review your dossier, and you will have my news shortly.

—Indeed, on the next day a telephone call from Dr. . . informed me that the authorization to resume publication of *Demain* would arrive in a day or two.

In fact, we did receive that authorization; it stipulated two conditions:

1) That we abstain from any political allusion;

2) That each month, after publication, we would send two copies of our Revue to the appropriate German authorities.

Due to this, we found ourselves face-to-face with a very cruel dilemma!

To refuse to reappear, when we now had the possibility of doing so, would be to condemn ourselves to inaction for several years—since a total Allied victory did in fact appear quite unlikely before 1945-1946, and in the still quite difficult conditions—to act in such a fashion would perhaps be to sacrifice deliberately everything that we had accomplished up to that time.

On the other hand, not feeling myself to be well adapted to the business life, I personally leaned toward republication, despite the loss of substantial material advantages that it entailed for me.

Finally, it was decided by a majority of the council to resume publication of *Demain*. The lot was cast!

Mr. Brihay, whose views turned out to be more and more personal and hostile, had cast a negative vote this time. A little while later, under a rather futile pretext, he had to submit his resignation as administrator. Thus ended, in an unforeseen fashion, a collaboration of many years.

The Revue *Demain* Under the Occupation

By accepting the task of appearing under the Occupation, we obviously did not deceive ourselves about the difficulties and the risks of that enterprise.

On the one hand, in fact, the sheep like public was inevitably going to black list us, believing that we were subject to German censorship.

On the other hand, the Occupation would fatally have its eye on us, and the day when their easy success came to an end, our situation would become perilous.

It truly would be—and I recognized it myself—playing a difficult game! But it is in my nature to take a chance; I think I have sufficiently demonstrated that already in this book. Easy successes have never interested me. "To conquer without peril, one triumphs without glory!" I have always said to myself, being the perfect Saturnian that I am. Besides, we believed that the Revue *Demain* had more than ever a mission to fulfill vis-à-vis our numerous supporters who had wanted to follow us up till now, because they appreciated our concern always to tell the truth, however disagreeable it was.

In addition, an internal instinct told me that without doubt certain circumstances would present themselves that could easily facilitate the task. And, once more, I had confidence in my star, although the MC of my chart had come at that moment to the square of Neptune and the semi-square of Saturn, which amply justified the difficulties or the moment, and did nothing to presage any better chances for the future.

In fact, everything that happened at the beginning went just as we had foreseen! In the eyes of some, our reappearance was considered to be a crime; we were believed to have sold out to the German propaganda machine, to have become slaves to it, and we were made to know this very often by means of anonymous letters. Some, however, had the courage to sign their missives, but these were, as chance would have it, members of spiritualist societies; they spilled out their thoughts in bitter and hateful words, and with such fury that there was something disgusting about it. Visibly, these people had never understood anything about spirituality! On top of that, some among them, seized by goodness knows what fears, were seen to come, under some hair-curling pretexts, to solicit the return of compromising correspondence. As we had no intention of embarrassing whoever it was, we magnanimously granted what they had requested. Besides, in that way we were certain to see no more of them.

In return, from the reappearance of the first number of *Demain*, modest as it was, and colorless even—it was necessary to sound out prudently the reactions of the German administration!—almost all our old readers had returned to us. And, little by little, the number of "sulkers" diminished, some among them even paid us a visit, some of them to inquire as to our exact position vis-à-vis the Occupation; the others to apologize for the expressions of blame that they had addressed to us.

It must be admitted, however, that our position was quite clear and without any possible equivocation; that position was exposed in detail in our first numbers during the war, and consequently, only those who did not read us or who only read between the lines could have been ignorant of it. Certainly, we set ourselves above the melee, in the interest of astrological verity, but we did not abdicate on that account, either sensibility, or concern for patriotism.

We affirmed that clearly and on several occasions. That one or another of our horoscopes, notably that of Marshal Pétain, had displeased certain readers, was the fatal thing; but my opinion was based upon astrological principles that were so evident that they seemed to me to be solid as a rock; so much so, that I would not change a word even today. And I could even say that the horoscope of Mr. Churchill that appeared in our columns, was, out of concern for objectivity, interpreted mechanically with the aid of Antarès's manual; certain passages that were too personal were, however, suppressed out of an understandable concern for tact.

Sometimes, I had some hard months, but those will understand me who deplore the fact that in time of war the soldier is relegated to the simple rank of "human material," that is to say, to the worst slavery that history has ever known. How much blood was thus stupidly spilled by the unconcern or the indifference of certain politicians!

I jump, of course, over a number of adventures to which I intend to return a little later; and I come now to a misunderstanding that suddenly aggravated our situation from a moral point of view.

That was the time when, in response to the encouragements of the Belgian Radio at London, the famous "White Brigades" began to strike against the Germans and the Rexists. An assassination attempt was thus organized at the seat of the Degrelle party, perhaps aimed at Degrelle[56] himself; but only one of his personal guards was killed. Naturally, some solemn funeral services were held for him, to which the value of a public atonement was given. The next day, one could read in the newspapers an account of that ceremony, and the names of the personalities that took part in it. Among the latter a Commandant Brahy was mentioned, someone

---

[56] Translator's Note. Léon Degrelle, Belgian politician, who in 1930 founded the Rexist Party, which became an anti-parliamentarian and Fascist political party. The Rexists won 21 seats in the Belgian parliament in the 1936 elections. After the Germans occupied Belgium in 1940, Degrelle collaborated with the German Occupation and Military authorities. He was, therefore, hated by many patriotic Belgians. When Belgium was freed in September 1944, he was condemned in absentia to death as a traitor. He then fled to Spain, where he spent the rest of his life.

with the same surname, whom I had been unaware of until then, and a man who, it seemed, had been a party to the drawing up of the "Real Nation."

There was a big outcry, and without the intervention of the other residents of our building, who guaranteed on their honor that we had no Rexist attachment, and that it was a matter of a regrettable confusion of names, our offices would perhaps have been sacked, and at least our windows broken out. During the course of several weeks, I had to fight to dissipate all the backward thought among our neighbors, friends, and relations. A year later, I was assured, in a broadcast emanating from the Congo, that the same confusion had occurred there, with threats of the settlement of accounts as soon as victory would be achieved.

That went on so long that I finally judged it indispensable to publish a notice in *Demain* in which I drew attention to the similarity of names in question, and that it could result in something disagreeable for me. But then there was another thing! I was summoned to appear forthwith before the German administration, where they asked me whether I considered the qualification of Rexist as infamous, as it would seem to follow from the text of my notice. I declared that, while not making any political statement, I did not want to undergo the consequences of an attitude that had wrongly been attributed to me, nor especially to receive blows that were intended for others, and which I had not provoked. I was judged not to have committed any important offense; and I was threatened with the seizure of the Review in case there was any repetition; but I was let off this time for having made some platonic injunctions.[57]

The German administration finished, moreover, by not taking very seriously the invectives to which my brutal frankness, and my quite Liègian stubbornness, sometimes inclined my pen. Already, when at the moment of emerging, I was asking myself about the

---

[57] Translator's Note. That is, for having made statements that had little or no effect.

kind of "surveillance," of which I could be the object, and whether some special directives might be imposed upon me, I was told: "Stay with astrological techniques, and all will be well!" And, as I had made plain my intention to publish some predictions relative to current events, as I had before the Occupation, the official in charge, horrified by this intention, which could never have been emitted in Germany, where all the astrological Reviews had been banned, had introduced me forthwith to his chief, a military man, but one who was relatively affable. He, in the course of a lengthy discussion that we then had, seemed to be very much amused by the stubbornness with which I was defending my point of view on astrological propaganda by an exhibition of cases. Finally, he got up, and, with the easy laugh of someone who surrenders to a whim, he said to me: "Do whatever you want to do, but take note that in that case your situation would become more uncertain, and you would be held answerable for any incidents or exaggerations that could result from your attitude."

And, when I asked him if there were definitely some subjects or some areas that were considered to be "taboo," he gave me this advice:

Do not say anything about Hitler or about your King, nor about the Jews; and do not in any case try to create any changes of public opinion. As for the rest, say what you see [as an astrologer]; it is not your predictions themselves that we fear, but rather the consequences that they could have among the public. We want to see the Belgians working in peace, and, as for the rest, not changing their customs in any way. Ah! And especially, no meteorological predictions, do you understand!

That was plain enough, insofar as their explanation was sincere—some reasonable enough demands, it seemed. Besides, one could see quite well how to contravene them or turn them aside, if one day the necessity presented itself.

It did precisely present itself in connection with Hitler's horoscope. In an article that appeared well before the War, I had already said that I had declared that the apogee of luck would present itself towards 1939. Now, the lightning successes won by Germany beyond that date no longer matched those forecasts. That is why I had been led to research the reasons for that discordance.

I found it in the existence of a parallel aspect between the Sun and Jupiter, which I had not taken into account, and which logically prolonged Hitler's luck into 1942.

Desirous of repairing that blunder, and especially the bad impression that it could have created, desirous too of rectifying my predictions with regard to the near future, in August 1941 I published a clarification of [my analysis] of the Führer's horoscope. I expected a new reprimand, since I was encroaching on forbidden territory, but nothing happened; no doubt, by promising again a certain period of luck for the German dictator, it could be believed by the Germans that that latest prediction allowed the necessary time to win the War. Perhaps too—and this is very much more likely—my article simply passed by unnoticed!

However, a complication troubling in another way presented itself two months later, when our French collaborator, Mr. Frédéric du Carpon, sent us an article in which he declared an opinion diametrically opposed to mine, and in which he openly declared that Hitler was already on the fatal downhill slope. We were really embarrassed at that moment. Objectivity commanded us to publish our collaborator's opinion; but on the other hand, by doing so we would be exposing ourselves to some severe sanctions, not just from touching on the person of the Führer, but especially from the fact of speaking of it in an unfavorable sense. We finally kept ourselves close in this thorny case to what had always been our line of conduct—to act as it was necessary to act, in good conscience, without worrying about the consequences. Mr. de Carpon's article was inserted, but with a heading that made a clear explanation of our attitude.

For several weeks we remained with our teeth on edge, expecting to be arrested or prohibited from publishing. But the reaction of the German administration was entirely different. The functionary in charge of our Review praised our sincere concern, but pointed out to us that it was scarcely an attitude that was likely to be pleasing to the public, and that it could certainly cost us some cancellation of subscriptions. In short, he showed himself to be very amiable and almost obliging.

To tell the truth, I had the impression that that functionary had wound up by feeling a sort of sympathy for us, since he had been able to follow through various vicissitudes the efforts that we were making to remain objective.

But I hasten to say that he did not act like a convinced Nazi, and I even believe that he was not of truly German origin. In addition to which, he spoke French and English with the same ease.

That kind of sympathy on the part of that unstrict functionary could arise also from the fact that on the occasion of our obligatory conversations we had had some epic discussions. Besides, at the end of the interview, that functionary never failed to make some clever joke or other to me on the subject of my role as an astrologer. Thus, at the moment of the entry of the Germans into Russia, in a jeering manner he asked me my opinion about the new campaign in the East.

I replied to him that although the moment of the attack had been well chosen, one factor must have been grossly underestimated, one that would bring some surprises.

—But when do you see victory for us? he asked me.

—Certainly not before the spring or summer of 1942, I replied. That is the most favorable hypothesis.

My interlocutor then burst into laughter, and advancing towards me, he said

—Three weeks to Moscow, Mr. Astrologer!

Later, when I reminded him of that response, he was evidently very sad, but I saw quite plainly that after that he felt himself to be in a state of inferiority to me.

He even ended by giving proof of an absolutely good disposition towards me at then time when, with the Führer's star declining, we made some allusions in the Review to some less favorable eventualities for the Axis Powers.

Do not make any statements that are too direct and that would attract attention, he recommended! Talk in paraphrases when you need to! Don't say anything about Italy; designate it some other way.

—The Adriatic peninsula, for example?

—That's right.

More and more I was persuaded by the existence of this attitude of the German services at Brussels, and by the rivalry that existed among the Occupation administrations from one town to another, that *Demain* could thereafter formulate prognostics unfavorable to the Axis as freely as it had done when the juncture was favorable to them.

One occasion had again confirmed this for me.

It was in the latter months of 1942; the situation in Italy was progressively getting worse, and we had let that be understood. One day, I was abruptly summoned by the German press services.

—Someone is angry at your Revue, the functionary said to me when he reviewed my case. Someone has denounced certain passages in your publication to the Central Press Service at Brussels, and this has been used as an pretext to request us to ban your publication. Personally, however, I will take no action, because I do not want anyone to believe that we are afraid of your revelations. But I cannot guarantee that I would be able to act in that way if an order of prohibition should come to us from higher up.

However, these fine promises did not prevent us from receiving, nearly every three months, a threatening letter directing us to reduce either the number of pages in *Demain* or else the size of its press run. Consequently, our Revue ended by being only a ghost of its former self.

But the coup de grâce was given to us in December 1942. We had just published our forecasts for the Year 1943, in which there was a question of the possibilities of peace or of an armistice on the side of Central Europe. Furthermore, in answer to the request of numerous readers who were concerned about the future of the Rexist leader, we had once more published the horoscope of Léon Degrelle. That horoscope had been discussed objectively; we had set forth the weaknesses of the chart and his very doubtful future prospects; but that judgment had been stated in a diplomatic fashion. In that way, those who before all else desired to know the truth were clearly satisfied; but as for those who hoped to find there some encouragement for the position they had taken, they would necessarily be disappointed, but they would not be able to accuse us of being partisan or of any systematic antipathy.

It seemed, however, that in the Rexist Party, they were strongly affected by the publication of that horoscope, which was undermining the recruitment propaganda used by that party. And, as the Central German Administration of the Press at Brussels, as has been seen, had initially turned a deaf ear to these complaints, it was by the Minister of Propaganda, Mr. Goebbels in person, that a new protest was introduced.

A few days later, there arrived from Berlin an order to prohibit our publication without any possible discussion. We were notified of this order by the Brussels authority, with many apparent regrets; and all that we got was permission to publish a final issue without any predictions of any kind, with a view to taking leave of our readers.

We experienced a very understandable moment of confusion; the affair could in fact become more complicated from one day to the next, for the complaint that was aimed at us gave rise to many grievances, notably of having brought to public notice some Masonic works (it was a question of ordinary reports of books that had been sent out as press services!) Also, various predictions unfavorable to the Axis were raised there, and notably our announcement of an armistice in Central Europe, and the one that fixed the year 1942 as the apogee for the Führer. Whatever could pass for favorable in 1941, quite evidently turned against us on the threshold of the year 1943.

It was, therefore, with a certain uneasiness that we were awaiting the sequence of events.

Happily, all this came to an end without any major damages. Our Revue having been eliminated from our activities, we turned our efforts towards our book [publishing], which was then going at full output, and thus we published several new editions from our backlog, along with some new works, some with the authorization of the German services, and others being waived from that.

It was thus that I was led to translate two novels of the famous English writer Sir E. Bulwer-Lytton: *The Coming Race* and *Zanoni*. the first of these dealt with occult force and the intra-atomic force "vril"; the second is a marvelous novel about initiation.

One might ask, "Where did we get the paper?" In part it was from the black market, in part from our own stocks. In fact, in 1941, our printer, Mr. Léon Wyckmans, had been arrested by the Gestapo for printing a clandestine newspaper. He was sentenced to nine years of forced labor and deported to Germany. All our stocks of paper had been seized; but we succeeded in convincing the Gestapo that the stocks belonged to us; and we were thus able to utilize them for our later editions, notably some of those works that I have just mentioned.

At the end of 1943, there even appeared an *Almanach 1944*, which resembled the Revue *Demain* like its own brother!

Meanwhile, our financial Bulletins had continued to appear; but the German restrictions, which forcibly paralyzed the free play of the market, more or less blunted the exactitude of our indications.

that publication finally became a rather thankless task; but it is necessary to render this homage to our subscribers—they showed themselves to be very understanding.

Then came the Liberation, and, contrary to all logic, the dizzy high cost of paper that forced on us an almost total stoppage of publication. We were obliged, as were many other enterprises, to improvise our operations from one week to the next.

At the moment at which I am ending this chapter, that abnormal situation still persists, although there are signs of a certain amelioration; but the outlook is far from being unconstrained, and some new difficulties have arisen to join the old ones.

The devaluation of the French franc has, in particular, cut us off from the French market, even without taking into account that we also had to add a new loss to what we had also undergone at the end of 1944 because of the blockage of funds in the bank. Besides, what will happen to our capital funds immobilized in France? Another problem! Finally, the restrictions on international exchange arising from every direction, are not such as to permit a Revue such as ours, which is distributed to the four corners of the world, to view the future with optimism!

Also, without taking into account that some jealous persons, whom the success of our Revue has always caused to lose sleep, are doing everything that they can to throw monkey-wrenches into our wheels of progress. There are no falsehoods, no detractions, and no hypocrisies that they would not employ if that could harm us!

Mr. Bauwens, whose name I have already mentioned in connection with the Brussels Congress of 1936, is particularly outstanding in this respect.

In a review that he pretends to have founded as a clandestine publication,[58] he has spoken of me in pejorative terms, characteriz-

---

[58] So clandestinely that only a few rare individual astrologers can recall having seen the two or three mimeographed pages that constituted the No. 4 that appeared at the moment of liberation. I am able to maintain from that fact, that in the matter of "resistance" we did better in the review *Demain*.

ing me as a "knight of industry" (*sic*), and slandering me in the most ignoble fashion. At the most, he has condescended to recognize me as "a certain commercial surface"; but he has accused me, if I understand him, of various base actions, which I hereby deny categorically. His bad faith and his inaccuracy result moreover from the fact that he has refused to publish any of the rejoinders, however mild, that I have addressed to him to protest against his accusations. But that has not prevented him from affirming that I have refused to submit myself to the judgment of my "peers" (*sic*). Indeed, if I had no objection in principle to explaining myself before some associates who were qualified and in particular impartial, one will understand that by reason of the procedures that I am going to relate, I would in fact experience a certain reluctance to recognize as my "peers" Mr. Bauwens and his friends who were in no way qualified to play the role of judges. But, more to the point, why didn't Mr. Bauwens reproach me during the German occupation, and not afterwards, as he is reproaching me today? He had the opportunity to do so, since he had at his disposal, he says, a clandestine publication. The gesture would have been more courteous and....more noble.

Besides, I strongly invite Mr. Bauwens, if he has preserved a copy, to re-read the letters that he wrote to me at the time of the Düsseldorf Convention. The least that one can say of this, is that Mr. Bauwens's opinions vary very opportunely according to the circumstances.

All this is sadly human!

Where does this lead us? I believe that, as far as I am concerned, the stars regard me with a more clement gaze than in the course of the latter years; but that still does not establish the fate of the Revue and of our Society, whose horoscope proved to be very precarious during the course of the year 1945.

In that succession of worries and difficulties, I had only a single moral satisfaction to note; besides, I am relating it without any kind of pretension.

During the German occupation, I have said that the Allies often launched important battles at those moments that astrology would have judged to be entirely contra-indicated. The attempted landing at Dieppe, for example, was undertaken under a Mars-Saturn square,[59] and it had even provoked a disabused commentary in *Demain*. Then, when the liberating offensive came, after the penetration of Avranches,[60] and when the Allies were halted on the Meuse, in Holland,[61] I had a presentiment that they would again pursue their effort at the wrong time. And indeed the battle fought by Allied airborne troops at Arnhem was launched under awful configurations, and in the end—it was inevitable—it was a veritable disaster.[62]

Before this lamentable defeat, which resulted in the useless massacre of thousands of elite soldiers, I was terribly upset, and in great haste I wrote a letter to Marshal Montgomery, in which I took the liberty of pointing out to him, for a good end to his subsequent operations, that the meteorological conditions that had provoked the upsetting of his plans, would be reproduced again on certain dates that I indicated. By way of an indication, I mentioned certain times in the past when the same configurations had coincided with spells of bad weather that had been unexpected.

---

[59] Translator's Note. A cross-Channel attack on Dieppe was made by 6,000 Canadian and British forces on 19 August 1942. It was a total failure. The Allies suffered 3,670 killed, wounded, and taken prisoner, along with the loss of landing craft, 27 tanks, and 106 aircraft. On that date there was an exact square of Mars and Saturn at 6:23 AM, followed by Mercury square Saturn at 10:26 AM, and Mercury conjunct Mars at 12:37 PM. No astrologer would have recommended a military attack under such adverse configurations.

[60] Translator's Note. Site of the decisive breakthrough of the American Third Army on 25-31 July 1944.

[61] Translator's Note. In addition to fierce German resistance, the Allies were halted by the lack of supplies, which had not kept pace with their advance.

[62] Translator's Note. Two American and one British airborne divisions were dropped near Arnhem on September 17, 1944. The British landed right in the middle of two German S.S. Panzer divisions. Fierce fighting ensued, lasting ten days, until the remnants of the Allied forces withdrew. The British 1st Airborne Division lost all but 2,163 of some 9,000 men, and American losses were less severe. Mars was separating from a square to Saturn and applying by trine to Uranus, which turned retrograde two days later. Again, it was a bad time to start a military operation.

I had sent this letter, I must say, purely for conscience's sake, but without having any illusion at all that it would reach a high place. I supposed that I was not the first to take such a step, and that one of two things had resulted: either some analogous offers had been used previously and so they would remove any chance for mine, or those offers had not been taken into consideration, and, consequently, there was truly little chance that mine would receive any attention this time.

Then, to my great astonishment, several weeks later I received a letter postmarked from the Allied General Headquarters, in which Marshal Montgomery expressed his thanks for the information that I had thus communicated to him.

Marshal Montgomery was perhaps the only one of the Allied generals whose almost Spartan kind of life, and whose spiritualist ideas, predisposed him to a certain indulgence with regard to astrology.

I really suppose that in any case he must have considered my advisories only in a purely indicative and documentary sense. But I truly take some self-satisfaction in noting that our science had been regarded with a certain condescension on the part of a man as esteemed as he is.

Bill and Statement of Profits and Losses

It remains for me, as a good accountant, to draw up a balance-sheet of my activities and the balance of credits and debits that derive from it.

Personally, and as far as I am concerned, I declare myself to be satisfied, despite some crossed-out entries. I have worked for a cause that I believe to be just and worthy of interest. If by chance it happens that I can reflect with some feeling of bitterness that accounting or business could have made a better fate for me from the material point of view, I easily console myself by saying to myself that I would never have collected the same moral satisfactions from another kind of work. And then, occultism has taught me to become a philosopher, to be content with little, and to appear to be satisfied with my destiny in every circumstance.

This affirmation will perhaps astonish certain people who easily suppose that astrology is a gold mine that rapidly enriches the man who practices it.

This is perhaps true when one doesn't feel any scruple to commercialize it—one should in this respect refer to the indications that I gave in a previous chapter—but one goes about it differently when one wants to maintain a scientific status and to practice his profession honestly. In such a case, one limps along, or one joins the two goals; and it is already very well so!

The illusions that are current about the output of astrological practice doubtless explain the failures experienced by those who, on the day following the liberation attempted to create a magazine or an organization analogous to what we had [already] created, despite the fact that the way was all marked out, and that it was sufficient to be inspired by what already existed. But those who made these attempts no doubt entertained excessive expectations, and probably did not know either [the necessity] of imposing the necessary sacrifices on themselves in the beginning.

Besides, they would perhaps have done better to try to find original work immediately. By doing that, they would have avoided being reproached as only pale imitators and of setting up some perfectly useless competitions, while they would have assured themselves at the same time of a more cordial reception on the part of the public.

It is known in this regard that A. Volguine, the congenial director of the **Cahiers Astrologiques** at Nice has never wished, even though he has been requested to do so, to introduce into his Revue certain sections that *Demain* has made a specialty of. In good fellowship, he felt perfectly that by doing so he would put his publication in direct competition with ours. He has consequently preferred to be and to remain himself; this integrity, far from working against him, has on the contrary made his *Cahiers* a publication to be highly held, and one that is rightly considered as one of the best, if indeed not the very best, of the astrological Reviews that have been published.

But again, no more in our science than elsewhere, success only smiles on those who know how to take a personal risk and who do not spare their efforts.

An astrologer's career is a more thankless one than might be thought; and the young students who dream of becoming professionals would do well to consider at length the following affirmation formulated by a veteran who speaks from experience.

Since I am going to bring up the subject of professionalism, now is the time to mention a reflection that is not lacking in interest. In fact, I have often asked myself whether, if in 1930 I had been well inspired to give up being an amateur astrologer and to abandon the professional career that I had followed down to that time. Certainly, I had made that decision with the express intention of no longer doing astrology exclusively; but I meant by that the astrological technique, the interpretation, the research work. In place of that, I have often been led to make the remark that a good part of my time—too important a part—was lost in the supervision or the execution of a thousand administrative details. It is not sufficient to create an action or to set it in motion, it is necessary to maintain it, to keep the wheels turning, to act so that in default of the maximum effort—impossible to insure in an enterprise like ours—the results are not inferior to the expenses invested.

Now, only with difficulty can one imagine the many anxieties and difficulties that require constant attention and create in the long run a veritable mental harassment. There is the mail—and the fact that some letters could be avoided if the public would pay more attention!—there are the visitations, the consultations, the telephone, studies to insure or to control, the financial bulletins, the necessity of following consistency, the orders, their execution, their billing, the due-dates—and all the clients not paying at a convenient moment!—the complaints. And at the same time, there is the Revue to put together, the proofs to correct, the pagination to establish, the conversations with the printer; without taking into account the conferences and everything that relates to the actual editions. The simple control of all of that obliges one to exert unceasing cerebral gymnastics, which leaves only a very short time for the actual astrological work.

Now, one of the great difficulties in an astrological office is the recruitment of qualified fellow workers. It is easy to find a bookkeeper, or a stenographer; but it is more difficult to hire a secretary trained in astrological practice and knowing how to type. However, there is no use to conceal it; to assure her livelihood in an astrological studio, it is necessary, not only that she know her part, but also that she knows how to play the keyboard of the typewriter skillfully; otherwise the output proves to be inadequate.

And then, it is necessary to deal with the character of every person! One is a bohemian type, fantastic, he will waste time at some moments and then try to catch up at others. If he wastes time too often, to the detriment of his production, he will have the feeling of being exploited, when he alone is the cause of it. He will perhaps display some intentions that are so unreasonable that an astrological enterprise entirely departs from the usual norm. In short, all the conflicts that threaten regular business run the risk of disturbing a studio of that sort even more.

Aside from some inevitable minor difficulties, I have for my part generally had occasion to be satisfied with my co-workers; it is true that one would have had difficulty in finding an office more "golden" than that of the Revue *Demain*! None of them, however, would have liked to find themselves in my situation, if I may judge from the fact that I proposed to all of them to take my place one day, and no one was ever willing to take it. But perhaps they were wiser that I to be unwilling to sacrifice the tranquility of their existence for responsibilities that were more honorific than truly remunerative!

No doubt, in this regard, I have let myself be too easily incited by circumstances to extend more than was reasonable an organization of which I had not immediately foreseen all the possible developments. It would have been more reasonable, from many points of view, to limit myself more. But each department had its own interest, both spiritual and material; the one was lucrative, and it sustained the general budget; the other had less return, but it ensured more services from a technical or moral point of view; the publications had their own importance from the point of view of science and propaganda. It would have been necessary then to entirely sacrifice the intellectual and commercial interest or indeed to put at the head of each department an experienced technician; but in the latter case, the costs would have far exceeded the revenues. It can be seen that it is a vicious circle!

One can suppose that in trying to increase the commercial revenue, by adopting certain methods called "boosters," one would have been able to get out of this dilemma. But experience has shown me that in these sorts of things, there exists a plateau that is very difficult to surpass, without taking into account that these American methods are out of place when they are not applied to strictly commercial interests. That is why only dynamism enables one to hold that very complex organism a little closer in one's hands—dynamism, united with a certain spirit of devotion, or, in certain circumstances, even of renunciation.

In that respect, I was able during nearly ten years of service to appreciate the spirit of understanding and dexterity of a virtually perfect secretary, who never shirked a task and always knew how to face up to the most complicated situations. It is thanks to her that my efforts were regularly able to attain their goal; she played a good part in the success of our projects. The tribute that I am paying to her here is pure justice.

The Viscount de Herbais de Thun, on his part, actively seconded my efforts from 1927 on. Always on the job, preaching confraternity and exerting himself, patiently collecting the least useful materials, he contributed in a remarkable manner to establishing the doctrine[63] and to tracing the history of the astrological movement.[64] One must be eternally thankful to him.

It is seen that in spite of all these difficulties and the inevitable disappointments, I was powerfully aided in my task, on the material plane as well as on the moral plane. My other co-workers, Messers R. Brihay, Antarès, B. Paque, L. Horicks, and Mrs. Michaux, and, after the war, Mr. I. Verheyen, have also done their best to assist within the limits of their time and their temperament.

---

[63] Translator's Note. Probably a reference to the Viscount's book, Synthèse de l'Interprétation astrologique (Brussels: Éditions de la Revue Demain, 1938). It includes even the most minor details.

[64] Translator's Note. This refers to the Viscount's monumental treatise, Encyclopédie du Mouvement Astrologique de Langue Française au XXme Siècle (Brussels: 1944). It is also remarkable that it was printed during the German Occupation.

I want to thank them too.

If my relationships with some of them were sometimes gloomy, let each one examine his conscience; reciprocal good will is necessary to resolve difficulties. And touchiness or excessive ambition does not go well with that!

In this regard, I intend to render thanks to my former co-worker, G. Antarès. As a result of misunderstandings, of certain purely calumnious stories, in which I believed myself able to have faith, he was for several years my declared enemy. But finally, disgusted by the lack of confraternity among astrologers, also indignant at certain scandalous maneuvers of which I was the object, he wrote me a letter with a high elevation of thought, to propose a reconciliation with me in the higher interest of astrology. Which I accepted with obvious joy!

Unfortunately, a great moral force and a fine objectivity were necessary to resolve such an attitude, which necessarily implied certain renouncements of self-esteem. That is no doubt why such gestures are so rare among astrologers!

At the time of finishing this book, my thankful memory also goes toward all those who, from near or far, in Belgium or elsewhere, collaborated with the Revue *Demain,* and contributed to give to it that vitality that always made it a success. They are numerous, but their merit must not be lost from view.

Nor should the Press be forgotten! At first, very hesitant with regard to us, even skeptical or scoffing, it made itself more and more understanding. Some timid articles on astrology appeared then here and there. Under the auspices of the Review *Solidra*, I was able to set forth my viewpoint on the I.N.R. I also gave several talks over the microphone of some private stations, notably on the Radio-Conférence. Finally, the sympathetic Brussels newspaper *La Gazette* opened its columns to me; it must be said that that newspaper counted among its editors an authentic astrologer, Arthur Michel, who on that occasion and on many others made things very easy for us. Astrology also owes him its heartfelt thanks.

My work at *La Gazette* was particularly regular during the course of the second half of the year 1933; I published a series of articles there looking toward a sound initiation of the public into astrology. the newspaper *Le Soir*, strongly reserved in general with regard to the occult sciences had some encouraging words for certain of our efforts, notably the Congress of 1935. On its side, the satirical weekly *Pourquoi Pas* [Why Not] echoed certain ones of my predictions, notably the danger of an accident that weighed upon King Leopold III during the course of his displacement abroad;[65] it also welcomed with kindliness the rights of reply that I addressed to some polemicists who had attempted to scold astrology in its columns. The review *L'Efficience* also inserted many echoes in which astrology was found to be presented in a prudent but objective manner.

Many other journalists also manifested a more or less marked sympathy for our ideas. It was not only at the *Indépendence belge*, in which I had been asked to furnish an astrological chronicle, that I was obliged to cease that collaboration, not having wished to bend my astrological views to the political interests of that newspaper. To do that, there was in fact no need to resort to an astrologer; a whimsical writer would suffice!

When I try to recapitulate all the experiences through which I have passed in the twenty years that my astrological career has passed through without interruption, I am sometimes tempted to conclude that I would have been able to avoid many complications if I had not practiced occultism at the same time as astrology.

Occultism—I took into account too late—is hardly adaptable to the developments of public life; it is rather made for discreet works

---

[65] Translator's Note. King Leopold III (1901-1983), having ordered the Belgium armed forces to cease fighting on 28 May 1940, was deposed by the Belgian Government in exile and was subsequently taken prisoner by the Germans and held until he was freed in May 1945. Some of his countrymen opposed his return to the throne, but after a national referendum he regained his throne on 27 July 1947, with the promise that he would step down when his son came of age. Four years later, he abdicated on 16 July 1951 in favor of his son, who became King Baldwin I (1930-1993).

of interiorization; and no doubt that is why the true adepts shun the world and retire into solitude.

I have said previously, or I have let it be understood, that the life of an occultist is traversed by experiences of an order that is almost opposed to those of the ordinary citizen. And that is understandable—the aspirations, the goals, and the points of view being entirely different between the two. The man in the street is generally sheep-like—he absorbs ready made ideas like a sponge; the occultist thinks for himself, and every reaction passes in him through the sieve of reason.

Little by little, astrology, which at the beginning of my career, appeared to me exclusively as a science, has taken on the aspect of a guiding mission for me. What purpose does prediction serve, if indeed it is not to draw from it the teachings that it offers, and to find how to orient mankind better to the way of progress and to a better future?

That is why, even before that great torment, I had raised my voice each time that it had seemed to me to be appropriate to give useful warnings to my counterparts. No doubt, those warnings experienced an uneven fate, but they were at least formulated with the sincere desire to be useful and from the awareness of my responsibilities.

Quite often, along that line, when I had to repeat them once more, I knocked myself against the wall of public opinion. When I announced in 1933 the extraordinary ascension [to power] of the Chancellor of the Reich—a man who would effectively become some years later a Messiah of an entirely diabolical kind—or when in 1939 I expressed my fears regarding the development of a war that everyone believed would be won in a few months; or even when, at the end of 1944, on the eve of the liberation, I sent a solemn appeal to the Allied Union to let them glimpse the very sinister clouds that darkened the end of the year 1945; every time, I felt that my warnings fell upon the public spirit like snow in the springtime. So great is the strength of illusions and of the hopes to which one attaches his reasons to live; so powerful is the virtue of inertia, which pushes us ceaselessly to relax, to enjoy life, and to grumble under the whip of destiny from that merciless executioner!

How many of my audience have thus left my lectures with animosity, with raillery, or even with malice in their hearts! But how many among them have returned later to make honorable amends . . . and to confess to me the antipathetic sentiments that they had felt towards me! It is among those that I still find today my most faithful sympathizers and my most sincere friends.

Two methods offer themselves to the astrologer: either to flatter his public and [thereby] assure his popularity to the detriment of the pure truth, or to proclaim that same truth, such as he sees it, and to bid adieu to material advantages and to easy fame.

Is it necessary to certify that at the Revue *Demain* it was that second attitude that always prevailed.! I do not say that to earn any merit for it; I have no merit by saying that; I took that attitude entirely naturally; it would have been impossible for me to act differently.

Also, when during the course of that war, our publication was able to reappear, I thought that more than ever I could not isolate astrology from its spiritual mission. And that is why I sometimes took a position in a sense that astonished some of our readers.

It was daring, even dangerous, to want, as I then did, to keep myself above the fray, to dismiss any consideration of propaganda, Allied or enemy, in order to keep my eyes fixed on events such as they actually occurred, rawly, without color or without any artificial fog.

It was daring, because the only country in the world in which that attitude could have been understood or allowed was practically isolated from us; and even if it had been otherwise, the mentality of free English thought would not have been able to forcefully impose itself upon the generally sectarian and petty mentality of the average Belgian.

It was daring, because it was difficult to make those who did not belong to an intellectual or moral elite to understand that that attitude did not necessarily exclude either sentiments of patriotism or common sense.

It was daring, because at certain moments the feeling of universal fraternity risked stepping on the national feeling, because losing to that degree all contact with the judgment of the masses, it was difficult at any moment to determine the gap that separated that judgment from my own.

Be that as it may, it was a very tough experience! Both materially and socially, I was sometimes inclined to regret it, for it brought me great troubles, and I sometimes had great difficulty in dissipating certain misunderstandings. Morally, by contrast, it was for me an infinitely precious time, and, as I believe that nothing happens without a reason, I have tried to draw from it all the amount of education possible.

Thanks to it, I have become more profoundly philosophical, more sensitive to human imperfections, and more desirous of remedying them. And Hermetism strongly attracts me anew, to the point that my love for astrology sometimes falters.

The scientific side of things has not ceased to interest me, but I feel myself more and more drawn by their human side. The moral sense is perhaps that which the war has attacked and obscured the most profoundly; it is there perhaps that it has exercised its most pernicious ravages. Now, of what use would it be to do any scientific work if that work must be utilized against man himself and against his happiness?

Already, one sees astrology turning its back on what it should be, on that which we would have liked that it was, falling back into the rut out of which we had drawn it and serving the most vulgar superstitions, the most common instincts. Almost all the monthly or weekly publications—some even daily—publish an astrological guide, whose value is scarcely more than that which one wants to attribute to it. Was it well worth the pain to make so great an effort to arrive at that?

That is not, it must be understood, to the authors of these guides that these disabused reflections are addressed. Most of them work conscientiously and also as learnedly as possible. But they know as well as I do that what they are doing—the indications that they are furnishing to the public are of too general a nature for anyone to be able to draw anything real from them.

Besides, certain ones of these chronicles contradict themselves quite curiously by nevertheless interpreting the same configurations and for the same moment! How does one wish after that for astrology to be taken seriously?

Also, one won't wonder that, some days, when I measure the time that has passed since the war in the astrological movement, when I see from where it would be necessary to start out again and where it would be necessary to succeed in order to attempt a correction, a sort of discouragement comes over me. Astrologers, the task that is before us is a very ungrateful one, and it will require on our part a veritable moral heroism if we want to protect the work that has been done up to now.

In any case, are the young able to be inspired by their elders in this field!

Also, the Press as a whole—which seems to have taken on astrology in order to grab the attention of the crowd—can it comprehend exactly its role and its moral responsibility! The result is, in fact, that our science has been corrupted into a kind of public amusement, and that its role—eminently social, philosophical, and human—finds itself brought to light by chronicles of quality. The public is, or remains, what the Press wants it to be, but it can also, under its enlightened influence, complete its instruction and its education. It is constantly declared, however, that it shows its appreciation and its fidelity to those who take care to dissipate its ignorance or to show it things as they [really] are.

A magnificent role is thereby offered to the Press. Will it decide to take it on? I earnestly hope so!

Postface and P.P.C.

The last time before delivering this to the printer, I am re-reading these "Confidences"! One last time I am asking myself these questions: am I doing the right sort of thing to publish these memoirs? Have I been justified in putting myself in the position of criticizing the astrological movement? Have I not done the wrong thing to put certain of my confreres in question, even indirectly and anonymously, and thus to risk rallying some movements of ill-temper, some temperamental differences, over which time would otherwise steadily let fall the mantle of oblivion?

However, the more I reflect, the more I am led to believe that such a focusing would not be superfluous for the future of the astrological movement. If, at the first glance, it provokes some irritable responses, on the second analysis it will give birth to some salutary changes of conscience, which will, sooner or later, bear fruit.

Besides, have I myself not attempted to give here an account of my own errors, and to contrast them with the results achieved? Having thus given proof, as much as was possible for me, of one of those qualities that I would like to encounter in all astrologers, I do not think that anyone can seriously reproach me for using the same right of judgment vis-à-vis others.

At the same time, I think that one will admit that my criticisms—which are often impersonal—are moderate and expressed with courtesy and objectivity. In short, I have taken care, as I should, to put a cap on my foil before descending into the lists. I do not in fact undertake an evening of accounts, but simply a kind of survey.

Perhaps one or more of those whom I have thrust at will judge himself to have been harshly singled out! It is only that I find myself in that case in a legitimately defensive state, and that I must face disloyal attacks. Besides, who sows the wind must expect to reap the tempest some day!

Although most often one sows discredit quite unconsciously, without taking any note of it, believing oneself to be sincere, because one has confidence in things that are commonly said, in idle remarks of jealous persons, or in deceptive appearances. Consequently, indulgence must more often assert itself than counter-attack!

Agreed! And therefore let it be well understood that in any case I have not wished to wound anyone who was like that, nor to exteriorize any rancor; for, I have no reflex of personal self-love that is obliged to give way before the well understood interest of the astrological movement. But still, it is necessary that these good intentions be shared, and that a reputation not be put at risk by calumnious attacks.

It is unlikely, moreover, that that unity of the astrological movement will see the day for quite a while; besides, some more urgent tasks presently require attention! The world, already quite sick since the First World War, is today falling into madness and imbalance. More than ever, all the good will is necessary to contribute to its moral recovery. Also, I have the impression that I could be more useful in the field of pure humanity than in trying at whatever cost to draw astrology out of the mire. Already for many years, I am hearing resounding in myself a more and more clear cry, which has finally taken the form of an imperious order.

Perhaps my friends are right: this war has marked the end of an epoch, and the times that will succeed it will in no way resemble those that have preceded it. Some times it seems to me that however much I feel impatient with new tasks, it is a new man that the war has made to be born within me, and one that little by little takes the position of being tormented by what I have known previously.

Everything that I have tried out and gone through, will it turn out to be only a prelude? And am I truly going, as I think I have a presentiment of, towards a new manner of life, towards what is perhaps very simply, life itself?

Index of Persons

Albert I, King of the Belgians (1875-1934) 169

Alcibiades (c.450-c.404) 119

Aldrich, Elizabeth (1875-1948) 105

Allendy, Dr. René (1889-1942) 110

Antarès (Georges Marcel Mostade) (1900-19) 78,85,110,185, 201,202

Antoine, Louis (fl. 1900) [founder of a Christian sect] 11 n.18

Baert, Miss 82

Bauwens, Robrecht (fl. 1937) 88-90,193-194

Bernoud, Georges-Louis-Marie (1903-19) 110

Besant, Annie (1847-1933) 41-42,52

Blanchard, André, Abbé (1899-1989) 109,124

Blavatsky, Helena Petrovna (1831-1891) 41

Bottelbergs [a Rosicrucian?] 56

Boutaric, Prof. 169

Boudineau, André (1891-19) 110

Brahé, Mrs. Gine 81

Brahy, Commandant (fl. 1941) 185

Brahy, Gustave Lambert (1894-1989) *passim* 103

Brétéché, Dr. (1900-19) 110

Brihay, Raymond (1898-19) 176,181,201

Brück, Remy, Major (fl. 1851-1866) 170

Bruknus, Walter (1904-1976) 104

Bucco, Mrs. 110

Buisset, Gen. (d.1927) 25,38,58

Carrel, Alexis (1873-1944) 169

Chapellier, Théodore (1888-1965) 33,35,38,41,58,64,85-86

Choisnard, Paul (1867-1930) 37-38,77

Churchill, Sir Winston (1874-1965) 185

Clancy, Paul G. (1897-1956) 110

Cognié, Henri (1879-19) 110

Conte, Mrs. (fl. 1937) 110

Cornell, Dr. Howard Leslie (1872-1938) 106

Coton-Alvart, Dr. (fl. 1937) 110

Courand, Henri-Robert (f. 1937) 110

Cox, Prof. [Belgian] 78

Crookes, Sir William (1832-1919) 167

Damiani, R. (fl. 1946) 84,110

Degrelle, Léon (1906-1994) 185,190

De Landtsheer, Octave François (1877-19) 23,33,35,38,58,77

Delaporte, A. [E. Delporte?] 84

De Luce, Dorothea (1897-1959) 84

De Luce, Robert (1877-1964) 84,93

Demain, Miss 69

Du Carpon, Frédéric mille (1842-1925) 188

Duff, Howard M., Sr. (1887-1979) 104

Duprat, Dr. Henri (1878-19) 110

Edward VIII, King of Great Britain (1894-1972) 116

Elizabeth, Mrs. (fictitious person) viii,97,102

Faery, Mrs. Tinia (fl. 1937) 110

Flammarion, Camille (1842-1925) 170

Fournier, Ed. (fl. 1937) 110

G—, Mrs. [an unidentified early member of the Institute] 62

Lagier, René (1894-19) 110

Lagrange, Ch. 6

Lantzsch-Nötzel, Arno Martin (1894-1986) [artist] 91,110

Lasson, Léon (1901-1989) 110

Leadbeater, C.W. (1847-1934) [Theosophist] 41-42,52

Léonard, Jean 41-42,110

Lechaut, Mrs. 110

Lecomte [journalist] 69

Loewenstein, Alfred (1874-1928) [financier] 71

Lytton, Edward Bulwer-Lytton, Baron (1803-1873) vii,192

MacNaughton, Duncan (1892-1973) [Maurice Wemyss] 83

Magi Aurélius (Hallet, R.) (1886-19) 81

McCaffery, Ellen (1886-1953) 105,110

Maillaud, Firmin, Col. (1865-19) 81,83,88,93

Mann, Harold (fl. 1950) 105

Medaets, Charles, Lieut. [military aviator] 38-39

Michaux, Mrs. Henriette (fl. 1946) 110,201

Michel, A. [journalist] 69,202

Montgomery of Alamein, Bernard L. Montgomery, Viscount (1887-1976) 195

Moulièras, Miss de [Mouliéras? – given both ways] 110

Mussolini, Benito (1883-1945) 116,169

Muysers, Paul (1899-19) 85

Ne(c)roman, Dom (1884-1953) 4 n.6,59 n.38

Nicolay 33,58,64

Nordmann, Dr. 169

Paque, Désiré-Boris (1899-19) 201

Parenty, Mrs. Andrée (fl. 1937) 110

Pascal, Mrs. Michelle (fl. 1937) 110

Pétain, Henri Philippe, Marshal (1856-1951) 185

Pezet 110